Ethel Meyer

A practical dictionary of cookery

1200 tested recipes

Ethel Meyer

A practical dictionary of cookery
1200 tested recipes

ISBN/EAN: 9783337149192

Printed in Europe, USA, Canada, Australia, Japan

Cover: Foto ©Lupo / pixelio.de

More available books at **www.hansebooks.com**

DAINTY DISHES

AT

SMALL COST

BY

A. M. MIÉVILLE

LONDON
A. D. INNES & COMPANY
LIMITED
1899

Dedicated

TO

ALL MY FRIENDS

CONTENTS

		PAGE
I.	SOUPS	1
II.	FISH	15
III.	ENTRÉES	33
IV.	JOINTS AND SIDE DISHES	55
V.	VEGETABLES AND SALADS	71
VI.	PUDDINGS AND SWEETS	83
VII.	SAVOURIES	105
VIII.	SAUCES, ICING, ETC.	121
IX.	HORS D'ŒUVRES	133
X.	FANCY BREADS, CAKES, ETC.	141
XI.	PRESERVES AND PICKLES	157
XII.	USEFUL HINTS	165

SOUPS

(WRINKLE)
Woman's special occupation, is the administration of her household.

How to keep a good Stock-pot for every-day Soups.

Put into a stewpan some onions, after first frying them brown, in a little butter. Then add any bones, from cold joints, chicken, or ducks; then add some carrots, turnips, a bunch of herbs, a little celery, three lumps of sugar, some pepper, salt, and a little allspice. Fill up the stewpan with cold water. Let all simmer for twelve hours, and then drain off all the liquor, and put into a basin to get cold. Remove the fat. From nicely made stock, good vegetable soups can be made. A good cook always has plenty of stock for soups, sauces, &c.

A stock-pot can always be kept going, as there are generally plenty of bones, pieces of bacon, &c., for it.

A stock-pot should be emptied every night, even if the same stock has to be furnished the next day. All fish bones and trimmings should be boiled down with water and spices, &c; and this stock is best for making white sauce, for serving with fish, or for moistening fish, for fish puddings, or fish cakes.

Clear Soup.

INGREDIENTS:

1 lb. shin of beef.
Knuckle of veal.
Plate of washed and sliced vegetables—onions, carrots, turnips, celery (or a muslin bag of celery seed).
Bunch of sweet herbs.
Spices and salt.
3 lumps of sugar.
2 quarts of cold water.
1 egg (white only).

First fry the onions in a stewpan, with some butter, until quite brown, then put in all the meat and vegetables. Add the water, and let all come to the boil, very, very slowly; then draw it to the side of the fire, and let all simmer slowly for six or seven hours. When you think all the goodness is out of the meat and vegetables, have ready the white of the egg, beaten to a stiff froth, and squash up the egg-shell. Put the white of the egg, with the shell, in the stewpan, and whisk it hard in the soup for a minute or two. Then let it all come slowly to the boil, and when the scum has all risen to the top, lift the stewpan off the fire, without shaking it, and pour the soup, very carefully, through a fine hair sieve, over which is a fine piece of muslin (mind the sieve is hot, by having hot water poured through it), and be careful not to pour it out fast, or shake. When it has all been poured off, it will be perfectly clear, like sherry.

To this soup can be added chili vinegar, or sherry, or any flavouring you may like, and when serving it you can have narrow strips of tender cooked carrots and turnips, and a few tarragon leaves in it—they look very nice in the clear, bright soup—or tops of asparagus or savoury. The bones and vegetables can be put down again, with less water, and this stock does very well for vegetable soups or *purées*.

Oxtail Soup.

INGREDIENTS :

1 oxtail.
3 onions, sliced.
2 ozs. butter.
2 sliced carrots and turnips, and a stick of celery.
Slice of ham or bacon.
½ pint of water.

2 ozs. of flour.
1 teaspoonful of Worcester sauce.
1 teaspoonful of mushroom ketchup.
1 teaspoonful of port wine.
Spices. Bunch of sweet herbs.

Fry all together the oxtail, vegetables, and butter, until a brown glaze is formed at the bottom of the stewpan. Then stir in thoroughly the flour, add four quarts of cold water or bone stock. Then put in the spices (which should be tied together in a muslin bag), with the bunch of sweet herbs. Bring all to the boil, and skim. Let it stew gently until the pieces of oxtail are quite done. Then take them out and cut the meat off the bones, and put on a plate ready for the soup. Strain the soup through a sieve into a basin, and put aside until quite cold. Then remove all the fat and put into a clean stewpan ; add the Worcester sauce, ketchup, port wine (and a little browning if necessary), then put in the pieces of oxtail and serve very hot.

Celery Soup.

INGREDIENTS:

Half a teacupful of whole rice.
1 quart of white stock.
2 heads of celery (cut very small).
Salt.
White pepper.
¼ pint of scalded cream.
2 lumps of sugar.

Boil the rice in the white stock, with the white parts of the celery and sugar, until tender. Cook slowly, and when the ingredients are soft press them with the liquor through a fine sieve. Stir the *purée* well, and beat out any lumps which may have formed. Season with salt and pepper, and stir the soup over the fire and let it boil gently for a few minutes. Add the cream, and serve.

Fried *croûtons* should be served with this soup.

Palestine Soup.

INGREDIENTS:

A basinful of sliced Jerusalem artichokes.
2 ozs. butter.
Few strips of bacon rind, scalded and scraped.
2 bay-leaves.
1 quart of white stock.
Pepper and salt.
¼ pint of scalded cream.

Peel and slice a basinful of fresh artichokes, and let them stew with the butter, bay-leaves, and bacon strips in a saucepan with a closely fitting lid. When all is soft, pour over them the white stock, and let all simmer for an hour. Rub them through a sieve, season with the pepper and salt to taste. Add the scalded cream, or half a pint of boiling milk, and serve.

Fried *croûtons* can be served with this soup if liked.

White Soubise Soup.

INGREDIENTS :

2 small Spanish onions.
1½ ozs. of butter.
1 pint of white stock.
3 ozs. of breadcrumbs.

Little bacon rind, scalded and scraped.
1 pint of boiling milk, or ½ pint of boiling cream.

Take the onions, peel and cut them into slices, and leave them in a stewpan, with a closely fitting lid, with the butter, until the onions are quite soft, without being coloured at all.

When ready pour over them the white stock, and add the bacon and breadcrumbs, and let all simmer gently for one hour. Pass the soup through a fine hair sieve, and crush as much of the onion through as possible. Boil the soup once with the milk or cream, and serve very hot.

This soup is very good made with the liquor in which rabbits or a chicken has been boiled.

Tomato Soup.

INGREDIENTS :

2 lbs. tomatoes.
2 turnips. 2 carrots.
1 onion. Stick of celery.
3 lumps of sugar.

1 oz. of butter.
1 quart of water or stock.
Salt and pepper.
Teaspoonful of chili vinegar.

Slice the vegetables and put them in a stewpan with the butter ; let them fry for ten minutes. Pour the stock or water over them; let them cook until quite tender. Then press them through a fine wire sieve into a basin, with the stock or water they were boiled in. Add a little salt, pepper, and chili vinegar to flavour nicely, and when wanted for use heat up and serve with fried sippets of bread.

Potage à la Monte Carlo.

INGREDIENTS :

Bread.
Caster sugar.
Salt.

Milk.
2 eggs.

Cut some thin slices of bread, and dust them with sugar on both sides. Toast them a nice light brown, and cut them into fancy shapes, such as fingers, rounds, crescents, and heart shape or diamond shape. Arrange them in the soup tureen with a pinch or two of salt, then pour over them boiling fresh milk, and thicken with the raw yolks of the eggs.

Potage à la Provençale.

INGREDIENTS :

8 cloves of garlic.
Bunch of summer savoury herbs.
Stock or water.

Pepper.
Sugar.
Olive oil.

Boil six or eight cloves of garlic and a bunch of summer savoury herbs in a stewpan of clear liquor; the boilings of a chicken or rabbit would do, or water. Put thin slices of bread in the tureen, sprinkle them with white pepper, sugar, and olive oil in proportion to the quantity of bread. Pour over all the liquor, without the garlic or savoury, and serve immediately.

Conger Soup.

INGREDIENTS :

Conger eel.
3 quarts of water.
Onions.
Parsley.

Herbs.
Peas.
1 pint of rich milk.

Put the head and tail of a conger in the water, with one or two onions cut in slices, a bunch of parsley, and herbs. Simmer till the fish is done to rags; season with salt and pepper. Then strain, and add peas or haricots, or asparagus tops, and one pint of rich milk. Simmer again until the vegetables are tender; throw in some marigold leaves, and serve at once. Very good.

Bonne Femme Soup.

INGREDIENTS :

2 lettuces.
1 cucumber.
2 carrots.
2 turnips.
2 onions.

1 stick of celery.
Chervil. Tarragon leaves.
Stock.
Bread.
Sherry.

Cut all up into thin slices and thin strips and pea shapes with a cutter. Fry all lightly in a little butter and two or three lumps of sugar. Have ready a nicely flavoured clear brown stock, throw in all the fried vegetables, and boil well. Cut some thin slices of bread into stars with a cutter, and put in the tureen. Put a few teaspoonfuls of sherry into the soup while boiling. Pour the soup over the bread in the tureen, and serve. Very good.

Potato Soup.

INGREDIENTS :

3 lbs. potatoes.
2 quarts stock.
Pepper and salt.

1 onion.
2 lumps of sugar.

Boil the potatoes and onion, and pass through a fine wire sieve. Mix with them two quarts of boiling stock, or milk and water; add pepper, salt, and sugar. Set it again on the fire and let it come to the boil. Just before serving add one gill of cream. Serve little fried sippets of bread with this.

Asparagus Soup.

INGREDIENTS :

1 pint of good stock (white).
Asparagus.
3 eggs (yolks).

3 lumps of sugar.
1 gill of cream.

Cut up the green part of the asparagus and put it to swell in a stewpan, with a sliced onion and the sugar. When tender, add the stock, and let all simmer until the asparagus is done. Then press all through a fine hair sieve and return to a clean saucepan; add any salt and pepper to taste, and the beaten yolks of three eggs. When all is thick and hot, add the cream, and if it is not a good green add a few drops of Marshall's sap green.

White Soup with Macaroni.

INGREDIENTS :

3 pints of good white stock.	3 yolks of eggs.
¼ lb. pipe macaroni.	Pepper and salt.
1 tablespoonful of flour.	3 tablespoonfuls of grated Parmesan cheese.
1 gill of cream.	

Take the stock, which must be well flavoured and free from fat; bring it to the boil. Cook separately the macaroni (which has been cut into inch lengths) until soft, but don't crush them, and drain them well. Mix the flour into a smooth paste with the cream, and add the yolks of eggs slightly beaten. Stir this into about half a pint of the stock. Pour this with the egg mixture into the rest of the white stock, and stir over the fire until the soup thickens, but it must not boil. Add the macaroni, and pepper and salt to taste. Just before serving, add three tablespoonfuls of grated Parmesan cheese.

A quickly made Soup.

INGREDIENTS :

1 lb. tomatoes.	Tablespoonful of Bovril or Liebig's.
2 large onions.	
1 oz. of butter.	1 pint of stock or water.
Yolks of 3 eggs.	2 or 3 lumps of sugar.

Slice the tomatoes and onions, put them into a stewpan, with the butter. Put on a tight-fitting lid, and let them stew until tender. Then put them through a hair sieve, into a basin. Put the yolks of the eggs into a lined saucepan, and mix in a small tablespoonful of Bovril or Liebig; stir in a pint of stock or water. Now pour in the tomato pulp, and let all get very hot, without boiling. Pour into a very hot tureen, and fried *croûtons* can be served with it.

Tapioca Soup.

INGREDIENTS:

3 large onions.
2 large potatoes.
1 tablespoonful of tapioca.
1 oz. of butter.

1 pint of water.
1 pint of milk.
Pepper and salt to taste.

Slice the potatoes and onions into the water, and boil until quite tender. When done, rub through a fine wire sieve. Then add the milk, butter, tapioca, and pepper and salt to taste.

Boil all again for fifteen minutes, and serve very hot.

White Onion Soup.

INGREDIENTS:

6 large onions.
1 pint of water.
1 pint of milk.

1 oz. of butter.
Pepper and salt to taste.

Slice the onions, and boil in the water until quite tender, and rub through a fine wire sieve. Then add the milk, butter, and pepper and salt to taste. Boil altogether again for ten minutes, and serve very hot.

Chestnut Soup.

INGREDIENTS :

1½ lbs. of chestnuts, skinned and blanched.
2 quarts of stock.
Salt and pepper.
¾ pint of cream.

Stew the chestnuts (after they are blanched and peeled) in the stock until tender; press them with the liquor through a fine wire sieve into a basin; if too thick, add a little more stock. Add pepper and salt to taste, and stir over the fire until it boils, and then add the cream boiling. Serve very hot.

Green-pea Soup.

INGREDIENTS :

3 pints of fresh green peas.
2 quarts of stock.
1 teaspoonful of caster sugar.
Salt and pepper.

Boil the peas, until tender, with some mint, and put a tiny piece of soda in the water to keep them a good colour. When they are quite tender, put them into the stock and boil until you can press them quite easily through a fine sieve, with the stock. Add the sugar, and salt and boil up again. Serve very hot.

Clear Soup.

INGREDIENTS :

4 ozs. carrots.
4 ozs. turnips.
4 ozs. onions.
Parsley.
Tarragon leaves.
Chives.
Chervil.
½ lb. meat.
2 or three egg-shells.
2 lumps of sugar.

For two quarts of stock, take the carrots, turnips,

onions, and chop up well. Tie in a bunch a little parsley (not chopped), about six tarragon leaves, a few chives, a little chervil, ½ lb. of any meat chopped fine, either cooked or uncooked. Put all these ingredients into a perfectly clean copper stewpan; also put two lumps of sugar, two or three egg-shells broken up small. Then put the stock (cold) on to all these things, and have the whites of one or two eggs whipped to a very stiff froth. Add this to the other things, and give it all a thorough good beating up; then put the stewpan on the fire, and let it come very slowly to the boil. Let it boil about two or three minutes. Draw the stewpan away from boiling, and let it stand for a little while; then put it by degrees—dipping it out with a cup—through a fine sieve, with a napkin on it. It ought to be perfectly clear and have a delicious flavour. Put it back into a clean pan, boil it, and serve. Before serving boil some asparagus tops in a little salt and water, and some peas, if in season; if not, a little carrot, cut very small, and a few tarragon leaves and chives, and add this to the soup.

II
FISH

Order has three advantages—it relieves our memory; it saves our time; and it preserves our property.

The causes of failure in frying are: first, an insufficient quantity of fat in the pan; second, putting things in to fry before the fat is hot enough; third, too much moisture adhering to the surface of things to be fried. The best frying is done by plunging the article to be fried entirely in boiling fat, therefore the cook should have a good stock of frying fat, which can be strained and put into jars when the frying is done, and covered to keep out the dust, reserving each sort for its especial use— one for meat, one for fish, one for vegetables, and one for sweets fritters, pancakes, sweet omelettes, &c.

Whitebait.

INGREDIENTS :

Whitebait.	Breadcrumbs.
Flour.	Lard or dripping.

DRY the fish carefully by shaking them about in a clean dry cloth—a few at a time is best. Then have ready in another cloth a handful of breadcrumbs and some flour. Throw in a few whitebait at a time, and when they are lightly covered with the flour and breadcrumbs, and each fish is separate, throw them into boiling lard or clarified dripping, and cook for about two minutes. Use a frying basket, as it is easier to get them out of the fat ; only do a few at a time, and mind the fat is quite boiling. Drain them on a sieve in front of the fire, and serve very hot with rolled slices of bread-and-butter, and lemon cut nicely. If for devilled whitebait, put cayenne pepper on them directly you lift them out of the boiling fat.

Fried Fillets of Lemon Sole.

INGREDIENTS :

Sole (filleted). | Breadcrumbs.
Egg.

Cut the fish so as to make eight fillets, and dry well. Egg and breadcrumb them carefully, and fry in clarified dripping or lard. Dish up neatly in a ring, and put fried parsley in the centre. Serve oiled butter and lemon juice, and a little cayenne pepper, in a sauce boat. Also bread-and-butter and cucumber.

Grilled Whiting.

INGREDIENTS :

Whiting. | Pepper and salt.
Butter.

Take some nice, fresh, silver whiting and split them open like a bloater. Sprinkle each with pepper and salt, and lay them in a Yorkshire pudding pan in front of the fire. Baste well with butter. Cook about ten minutes, and dish up on a fish paper. Decorate with parsley. Any sauce can be served with this.

Fish Pie.

INGREDIENTS :

Pieces of fish. | $\frac{1}{2}$ pint of milk.
Eggs (4 or 5). | Few oysters or sardines.

Cut any solid fish into neat pieces—it must be free from skin and bone. Mix a seasoning of finely shred parsley, powdered marjoram, salt and pepper. Strew this over the fish, dip the pieces into warmed butter, and lay in a pie-dish, not too closely together. Beat four or five eggs well, and mix with half a pint to a pint of milk or cream. Put halved oysters or sardines between the fish, then pour the cream over. Cover with light pastry, brush it over with egg, and bake.

Sole à la Cannes.

INGREDIENTS:

Large sole.	Lemon-juice.
Breadcrumbs.	Chopped parsley.
Butter.	Cayenne pepper.

Cut the head off a nice sole, and cover with breadcrumbs and butter. Then bake in a brisk oven, and baste the whole time with lemon-juice, chopped parsley, butter, and cayenne pepper. Dish up very hot, and garnish with lemon cut in fancy slices.

Brandade of Cod.

INGREDIENTS:

2 lbs. of cod.	1 gill of milk.
Salt and pepper.	3 ozs. of butter.
1 pint of salad oil.	

Soak the cod, for at least twelve hours, in several waters. Boil it well, then pick it from the bones and skin. Chop it up very fine and pound it well; add pepper and salt to taste. Pour in the salad oil, drop by drop, keep stirring the same way. Put it in a saucepan, add the milk and butter, and continue to beat until quite hot; it should be of the consistency of cream cheese. Press it into a buttered mould, and turn out.

Fish à la Mièville.

Ingredients:

Fillets of sole, or whiting or brill.	Pepper and salt.
Butter.	Chopped parsley
Flour.	Milk.

Put the filleted fish into a baking dish, and upon each fillet put a small lump of butter, dipped well in flour. Sprinkle well with pepper and salt and the finely chopped parsley. Just cover them with milk, and put them in a hot oven until done, about fifteen minutes. Then dish up the fillets on a very hot silver dish, and keep them hot while you make the sauce, which is done by putting the milk, &c., that the fish was cooked in into a small saucepan, with a little shrimp or anchovy sauce. Stir in a spoonful or two of cream. This is very good.

Oyster Soufflé.

Ingredients:

3 ozs. flour.	Liquor from the oysters.
3 ozs. butter.	Dessertspoonful of anchovy.
1½ pints of milk.	6 eggs.
20 oysters, chopped and bearded.	Lemon-juice.
	Cayenne pepper and salt.

Mix the flour and butter smoothly over the fire,

add the milk, and stir until it boils and thickens. Pour half the sauce aside in a basin, add to the other half the oysters, chopped and bearded, the butter, liquor from the oysters, the anchovy, lemon-juice, pepper and salt. Mix all well together, stirring in the yolks of four eggs, well beaten. Then add the whites of the six eggs, beaten to a stiff froth. Butter a soufflé mould, tie a piece of buttered paper round it, and pour in the mixture, which should half fill it or little more. Steam one hour and a half. Serve very hot.

To use up remains of Cold Fish.

INGREDIENTS:

| Remains of cold fish. | Mashed potatoes. |

Make a nice melted butter and flavour with anchovy sauce or Worcester sauce, pepper, &c. When quite hot put in the remains of the cold cooked fish, which has been cut up into small pieces, dish up in the centre of a silver dish, and put a wall of mashed potatoes (slightly browned with salamander) round. Throw a sprinkling of chopped or fried parsley over. Serve bread-and-butter and cucumber with this.

Salmon Creams.

INGREDIENTS:

Remains of cold salmon.	Mushrooms.
6 tablespoonfuls of cream.	Pepper and salt.
2 hard-boiled eggs.	

Pound up the salmon, freed from bones and skin,

with the cream, in a mortar, and pour through a fine sieve. Put it back in the mortar, and add the eggs. Salt and pepper to taste. Butter some tiny fancy moulds, and sprinkle with chopped truffles. Fill up the moulds, and steam in the oven for half an hour. Turn out carefully, and put a hot mushroom on the top of each mould. Serve in a silver dish. Hand bread-and-butter and cucumber, cut very thin, with this dish of creams.

Salmon Mayonnaise.

INGREDIENTS:

Slice of salmon.	Cucumber.
Mayonnaise sauce.	2 hard-boiled eggs.
Endive. Lettuces.	Little coral.

Boil the salmon carefully (a nice slice about 2 lbs. makes a pretty dish), put it in the centre of a dish, and mask over with thick mayonnaise sauce, made from recipe No. 29 in Sauces. Cut up a fresh cucumber in thin slices, and arrange round the edge of the dish, one piece overlapping another. Then between the fish and cucumber put fresh-pulled leaves of endive and French lettuces (not cut with a knife), and little fancy cut pieces of hard-boiled egg. Sprinkle over the top of the salmon, just before sending to table, some coral from a lobster, which will keep in a tin if well baked, for decorating with. This is very nice for a cold luncheon or supper dish.

Lobster Cutlets.

INGREDIENTS :

Lobster.
Mace.
Pepper and salt.

Anchovy sauce.
Butter.

Take all the meat from a lobster and pound it up in a pestle and mortar with the mace, pepper, salt, and a few drops of anchovy sauce. While doing this, have all the shells of the lobster stewing in a little water or milk, with pepper and salt. When quite cleaned of all their goodness, pour it over the lobster in the pestle and mortar and mix all together, adding a little butter. Mind and pound in the lobster coral, so as to give the mixture a nice colour. Put all into a plate, and leave for a few hours until set, then take enough of the mixture and form into the shape of a cutlet, and finish off the thin end with the claw of the lobster. Egg-and-breadcrumb twice and fry in boiling fat ; drain carefully, and dish up on a bunch of fried parsley in a silver dish. Hand bread-and-butter with them.

Haddock Balls.

INGREDIENTS :

Remains of dried haddock.
1 gill of cream.

Pepper and salt.
1 egg.

Pound up finely in a mortar the fish. Add the cream, pepper, salt, and the egg. Make into a paste and leave to set on a plate. Just before cooking form the paste into little balls, and egg-and-breadcrumb each carefully. Fry in boiling fat until a nice golden brown. Serve each ball on a ring of freshly fried bread, place a haddock ball in each ring. Send fried parsley, heaped up, in the centre of the dish, or a pyramid of mashed potatoes, garnished with strips of anchovies and fresh parsley on the top of the pyramid. Any nice sauce is an improvement, such as mayonnaise or Hollandaise.

Fish Mould.

INGREDIENTS :

Remains of cold fish.
2 or 3 hot potatoes.

Melted butter.
1 egg.

Put the remains of the fish through a fine wire sieve. Flour to your liking, then put through the sieve the hot potatoes, and mix all with about two gills of melted butter and the whole egg. Mix well, and put the mixture into a fancy mould, or plain if preferred, and steam twenty minutes. Turn out in centre of a silver dish, and pour melted butter, coloured pink, over the mould, and garnish with parsley. Hand cut cucumber and bread-and-butter with this dish.

Haddock Sauté.

INGREDIENTS :

Fresh haddock.
Butter.
Capers.

Lemon-juice.
Sauce.

Take a nice fresh haddock, split it down the back,

and take out the bones. Season the fish with pepper and salt, lemon-juice, and finely chopped tarragon, and a sprinkling of tarragon vinegar. Place it in a well-buttered baking tin, and put a few small lumps of butter here and there on the fish. Cover the fish completely over in a well-buttered piece of foolscap paper, and put it in a moderate oven and bake for twenty minutes. Take it up very carefully and lay it on a hot dish and serve with ready chopped capers or gherkins and sauce round it (recipe given), which must be made and ready.

Fish Castles.

INGREDIENTS:

Lobster coral.
Capers.
Truffles.
Butter.
Anchovy sauce.

Remains of any cold cooked fish.
2 eggs.
1 gill of cream.

Well butter some small dariole moulds, and sprinkle chopped truffles, capers, and lobster coral all over the insides of the moulds. Have ready the remains of any cold cooked fish, pounded up in a mortar. Add pepper, salt, two eggs, one gill of cream, and a flavouring of anchovy sauce. Mix all well, and nearly fill the moulds. Put them to poach in the oven, with water round them, for half an hour. Turn out carefully in a silver dish, and pour round them a very nice shrimp sauce, and hand cut cucumber and brown bread-and-butter with them.

Whiting à la Horsell.

INGREDIENTS:

Whiting.	Pepper.
Oiled butter.	Breadcrumbs.
Lemon-juice.	Cucumber.

Steam the whiting, and when quite done remove the flesh from them carefully and throw into hot oiled fresh butter, to which must be added lemon-juice and pepper. Take some little white china fireproof moulds and fill each with the whiting and oiled butter; sprinkle a few fresh breadcrumbs on the top of each, also a piece of butter. Set them to poach in a pan half full of water in the oven until a golden brown. Serve in a nicely folded napkin in a silver dish and garnish with cut lemon, and hand brown bread-and-butter and cucumber with them. Delicious.

How to Fry Smelts.

Dry the fish carefully, and then roll in flour, wipe off all superfluous flour, and egg-and-breadcrumb twice. Have plenty of boiling fat. Fry two or three smelts at a time in a frying basket, and see they are well browned. Drain on a sieve in front of the fire and dish up crossways. Serve oiled butter and lemon-juice with them.

Cod à la Capers.

INGREDIENTS:

Slice of cod.	Lemon-juice.
Capers.	Butter.

Melt about $\frac{1}{2}$ a lb. of fresh butter in an enamel pan, add a good spoonful of finely chopped capers, and some cayenne pepper and lemon-juice. When all is quite hot and oily, lay in the slice of cod and leave to steam until tender. Take up carefully, and put aside to keep quite hot while you add a little more butter to that the cod was steamed in and a little flour. Stir all until it thickens, then dish up in a silver dish, the cod on a bank of mashed potatoes, and entirely cover the fish with the caper sauce. Hand bread-and-butter and cucumber with it.

Sole à la Nice.

INGREDIENTS:

Sole.	Salt and pepper.
Mushrooms, parsley, eschalot (chopped finely).	Slice of bacon, cut into small pieces.
Breadcrumbs.	Butter.

Mix together the mushrooms, parsley, eschalot with a tablespoonful of breadcrumbs; add salt, pepper, and the pieces of bacon. Butter a fireproof dish, and lay the seasoning on it. Put in the sole, and sprinkle with good fish stock. Put over all the breadcrumbs, and place little bits of butter on top, and bake slowly. Serve white sauce with it, and garnish the fish with fresh, fried parsley.

Fish au Gratin.

INGREDIENTS:

2 ozs. butter.	½ pint of milk.
2 tablespoonfuls of flour.	Pepper and salt to taste.
2 ozs. of grated cheese.	

Put the butter and flour into a saucepan to melt,

and then stir in the the cheese and milk. Boil for three minutes. The sauce should be the consistency of cream. Pour over any kind of cold fish, and bake in a moderate oven for quarter of an hour.

Fish à la Jess.

INGREDIENTS :

Fillets of soles, whiting, or haddock.
Chopped parsley and chives.
Breadcrumbs.
Teacupful of milk.

2 tablespoonfuls of Worcester sauce.
Half a glass sherry.
Butter.

Put the fish into a buttered baking dish, with the chopped parsley and chives, and the breadcrumbs sprinkled over. Then pour round the milk, Worcester sauce, and sherry. Bake in a brisk oven for ten minutes, and baste continually. Serve with all the liquor thrown over, dished up nicely in a silver dish.

Filleted Plaice.

INGREDIENTS.

2 ozs. of butter.
Filleted plaice.

Chopped herbs.
Salt and pepper.

Fillet the plaice and roll each one up; add salt, pepper, and chopped herbs, and a lump of butter. Put it all into a jar, with the lid on, and let it cook in the oven, in its own moisture, for ten minutes

Fillets of Soles à la Italienne.

INGREDIENTS :

Filleted soles.
Butter.

Pepper and salt.

Lay the fillets on a tin with plenty of butter, pepper, and salt. Place a sheet of oiled paper over them and put in the oven about five or six minutes before they are wanted, or they may be laid in a deep plate, in the same manner, with another one on the top of it. Then dish up neatly, and pour the following sauce over them :—

Sauce—Mince two eschalots quite fine, and fry in a little salad oil until they are a pale straw colour. Then add two or three mushrooms and a little minced parsley. Moisten with enough stock and white wines, in equal parts, to make the sauce. The stock should be made from the bones and skins of the soles boiled down in water or milk. Put in, tied up in small bunches, a sprig of garlic, some sweet herbs, and a bay leaf. Add pepper and salt to taste, and let the sauce boil for half an hour. Remove the bunch of herbs, and melt a small piece of butter, add a little flour to it, then the sauce, stir it well, and make very hot.

Soles à la Paine.

INGREDIENTS :

1 sole boned and filleted (lemon sole will do).
Onion or chives chopped fine.

Lemon-juice.
Pepper and salt.
Butter.

Have a sole boned and filleted ; rub each over with

onions or chives, lemon-juice, and pepper. Press the fillets together, forming the sole again. Have ready a flat fireproof dish. Place the sole in the dish and cover with sauce, and put a few lumps of butter on the top. Put the dish in a hot oven for a quarter of an hour, and before sending it to table garnish it with fried parsley and fancy-cut pieces of lemon.

Sauce for Fish.—Make a pint of melted butter, then add the yolks of two eggs, well beaten, and stir quickly over the fire until it thickens, but don't let it boil. Flavour well with pepper and salt, and it is ready for use.

How to Boil Dried Haddock.

INGREDIENTS:

| Haddock. | Milk. Butter. |

Put a deep frying-pan over the fire with enough milk to cover the haddock, and boil until tender. Then take it out, and place before a clear fire for a few minutes, with some lumps of butter on top.

Duncroft Soles.

INGREDIENTS:

| Filleted sole, or lemon sole. Chopped onion and parsley. Pepper and salt. | Chili vinegar. Butter. |

Take a filleted sole, rub over with the chopped onion, parsley, pepper, and salt, and a few drops of chili vinegar. Roll each fillet up, and skewer with thin game skewers. Put them in a baking pan, with a buttered paper over them, and a little butter in the pan. Poach in the oven for ten minutes. Take up, and dish each fillet on a round slice of hot tomato, and place a little piece of fried parsley on the top of each fillet. Serve oiled butter, with chopped capers, in a tureen. This makes a very pretty luncheon or dinner dish, having the three colours—red, white, and green.

How to Cook Salmon.

Put the fish into boiling water, and leave the lid off ; boil until tender. If to be served cold, let it remain in the water, after it is cooked, until cold.

III

ENTRÉES

(WRINKLE)

Economy is a virtue in poverty, a prudential measure in moderate circumstances, and a vice in opulence.

Fillets of Beef.

INGREDIENTS :

3 to 4 lbs. of fillet of beef.   Carrots, peas, and mushrooms.
Butter.   Green butter.
Pepper and salt.   Glaze. | Horseradish.

TAKE the fillet and cut into thick slices about two and a half inches across and about one inch thick, and allow a nice piece of fat to each. When ready to cook fry lightly in butter, about ten minutes; pepper and salt them before frying.

Have ready a bed, or wall, of mashed and nicely flavoured potatoes, arranged in a round silver dish. Have a little glaze dissolved, in a jam pot, and before dishing up the fillets put a teaspoonful on each to make them look a nice brown. Make a good brown gravy and pour round them (Recipe No. 10). Then have the vegetables nicely cooked, and cut in tiny balls or strips, and green peas to fill up the centre with, and ornament each fillet with green butter and freshly scraped horseradish, or if preferred send mushrooms in place of other vegetables. This is a very favourite *entrée*, only all the etceteras must be ready, so as when it is time to dish up nothing is forgotten or cold.

Stuffed Larks. (*Cold.*)

INGREDIENTS:

Larks (boned), one for each guest.
Pate de fois gras.
Mustard and cress.
Beetroot.

Take the larks, and stuff them with the pate de fois gras, and sew up carefully to form their shape. Stew them for three-quarters of an hour slowly in butter, and when cold glaze each one. Serve on a bed of mustard and cress, and chopped beetroot sprinkled over each, and fancy-cut slices of hard-boiled egg.

Chicken Cutlets.

INGREDIENTS:

Remains of cold fowl, or game.
Pepper and salt.
White sauce.
1 egg (the yolk only).
Breadcrumbs.

Take the remains of the chicken or game, and mince up very finely with a tiny bit of chopped onion; add pepper and salt and a little drop of Worcester sauce. Moisten with freshly made hot white sauce, and the yolk of the egg. Put away to set. When quite set, take up and form into the shape of cutlets. Egg-and-breadcrumb, and fry a nice golden brown. Put a stalk of parsley at the small end of the cutlet (to form the bone), and dish up on a long border of mashed potatoes, down the centre of a narrow dish, the cutlets overlapping each other a little. Pour a lovely mushroom sauce round—if mushrooms cannot be had, send tomato, or rich white sauce. Serve very hot.

Little Fancy Chicken or Game Moulds.

INGREDIENTS:

Aspic jelly.
Remains of chicken or game.
Cold tongue, or ham.
Hard-boiled egg.

Chopped parsley, chives, and tomatoes.
Tomato sauce, and gravy.

Prepare some little moulds, and brush over the insides with the white of an egg, and sprinkle over each, separately, the chopped-up white and yolk of the hard-boiled egg, parsley, and chives. Sprinkle all round the moulds well. Then put in the following mixture, and fill up each mould with warm aspic jelly. Set aside to get cold. Turn out each carefully, on to a nice lettuce and endive salad, which is first covered with thick mayonnaise sauce, coloured in strips of green, red, and the rest yellow.

The mixture.—Mince up the chicken or game, a slice of ham or tongue, and the insides of ripe tomatoes, pepper, salt, and moisten with a little gravy or tomato store sauce (Recipe No. 12). Do not make the mixture too moist.

Oxtail à la Cannes.

INGREDIENTS:

Oxtail.
Butter.
Bunch of sweet herbs.
Onion, stuck with cloves.

Pepper and salt.
Stock.
Celery.

Hash and divide into pieces the thin end of the oxtail, and fry in butter, in a stewpan, until well browned. Add a pint of stock, the sweet herbs, onion, celery, pepper and salt. Put the lid on, and let all simmer for four hours, very slowly. On no account let it boil. Take out the pieces of oxtail carefully, and put aside while you make a rich glazed gravy in the following way:—Strain the stock that the oxtail was cooked in through a tammy, and take off any fat with a piece of paper. Put in a little glaze, and a tablespoonful of mushroom ketchup, and flavour well. When quite hot, and a good dark brown colour, put in the pieces of oxtail to get quite hot. Dish up in a silver dish carefully round a mould of prettily cut and nicely cooked carrots, turnips, peas, or French beans.

Pigeons in Cases.

INGREDIENTS:

Pigeons.
Pepper.
Orange-juice.

Chili vinegar.
Red-currant jelly.

Take some young pigeons, bone them, and chop up all the meat from them into small dice pieces. Mix them with a little pepper, orange-juice, chili vinegar, and a little red-currant jelly, or sugar. Fill some little china ramequin cases with this mixture, and put them in a baking tin half full of water, and allow them to poach for twenty minutes. Just before taking the cases out of the oven, put a few breadcrumbs and a piece of butter on each, and when the breadcrumbs are brown, take up and serve in a silver dish, with a blanched leg of a pigeon standing out at the top of each case. Hand a tomato *purée*, in a sauce-boat.

Sweetbreads à la Hatch. (*Cold.*)

INGREDIENTS:

Tomato *purée*.   Sweetbreads.
Truffles.

Half fill (the number required) some white china ramequin cases with tomato *purée* (Recipe No. 15), and then fill up each with cold, blanched, cooked sweetbreads, and sprinkle each with cut truffles. This is also very nice, made hot ; and substitute chicken, cold game, or any hot meat, for the sweetbreads.

Jubilee Kidneys. (*Very good.*)

INGREDIENTS:

Sheep's kidneys.   Parsley.
Chopped chives.   Butter.
Onions.

Take as many sheep's kidneys as you have guests. Skin them, and cut in half lengthways. Rub each piece over with chopped chives, onion, and parsley. Put them in a pudding basin, with plenty of butter, and put them to poach in the oven, with a plate on the top of the basin, for twenty minutes. Dish up each kidney on a fried piece of bread, in a circle round a silver dish, and hand bread-and-butter.

Bantams' Eggs in Aspic.

INGREDIENTS:

Bantams' eggs.
Aspic jelly.
Tarragon leaves.
Truffles.

Tomatoes.
Anchovies.
Salad.

Boil some bantams' eggs hard, and peel them carefully. When cold, put some aspic jelly, nicely flavoured, into some small dariole moulds. About half fill them. Next put in the egg, some tarragon leaves, chopped truffles, and tomato. Turn out the next day by just putting the moulds into hot water for a second, and serve them in a silver dish, with lettuces and endive round, and boned anchovies. Decorate with beetroot.

Vol-au-vent à la Toulouse.

INGREDIENTS:

Puff paste.
Cooked game.
White sauce.

Olives.
Mushrooms.
Pepper and salt.

Have ready a nice hot puff paste vol-au-vent case, (not too large). Mix up some neat pieces of cold cooked game, made hot, in a thick white sauce, well flavoured, also some little forcemeat balls, stoned olives, and mushrooms. Fill up the case, and put the small lid of pastry on the top. Serve very hot.

Œufs poches au Asperge.

INGREDIENTS :

Eggs.
White sauce.
Tomato sauce.
Asparagus.

Boil some fresh eggs lightly, as many as required, and while hot carefully peel them. Place a slice of hot fried bread (cut round) in a dish, and place the eggs on it, and pour over them a thick white sauce, then a thick, hot tomato sauce round the edge and in the centre of the eggs. Cut up cooked asparagus, or any green vegetable, and put round, and serve up very hot. This is nice for breakfast.

Oysters en Caisse.

INGREDIENTS :

Oysters.
Butter.
Chopped chives.
Lemon-juice.
Cayenne pepper.
Breadcrumbs.

Take as many small white china cases as required, and place in each a piece of fresh butter, a little chopped chives, a few drops of lemon-juice, and a little cayenne pepper. Then put in one or two nice bearded oysters, and fill up the cases with fine breadcrumbs. Add a piece more butter, and a few drops more of lemon juice, and put the cases in a baking tin (with edges) half full of water. Place in a nice hot oven, and allow them to poach for about five minutes. Dish up on a folded napkin, in a silver dish, and garnish with fresh parsley, and hand a plate of new bread-and-butter, cut very thin and rolled.

Oysters in Mayonnaise.

INGREDIENTS:

Oysters.
Mayonnaise sauce.
Lemon-juice.
Cayenne pepper.

Hard-boiled eggs.
Fresh salad, lettuces, endive, radish.

Open the oysters carefully, and beard them. Keep the deep oyster shells, and place in each shell a teaspoonful of very nice, thick, mayonnaise sauce. Next place the oyster on the sauce, and flavour with lemon-juice and cayenne pepper. Then cover the oyster with mayonnaise sauce, and smooth over with a wet palette knife. Garnish each with the yolk of a hard-boiled egg, put through a sieve, then the white of the egg, also passed through a sieve, and a small piece of parsley on the thumb side of the shell. Dish on a napkin, or on a bed of endive and French lettuces pulled, and little red radishes between.

Crepinettes of Lobster (or of Meat, Chicken, or Game).

INGREDIENTS:

Flour.
Salt.
Dripping (or lard).

Water.
Eggs.
Parsley.

Make a paste of flour and salt, and either beef dripping or lard, and a little water. Roll out very thin, and cut the paste out with a round cutter. Spread one half with the lobster, or meat or chicken, which is first prepared as for cutlets. Then fold over the other half, and fasten the edges with a little water. Brush the crepinettes over with a beaten egg, and cover them with vermicelli broken small. Then fry them in boiling fat in the basket, and be sure the fat is deep enough in the saucepan to cover them. Serve in silver dish, garnished with bunches of fried parsley.

Lobster à la Mont Fleury (cold entrée or luncheon dish).

INGREDIENTS :

Aspic jelly.
Truffles.

Lobster butter.
Hard-boiled eggs.

Line a mould with aspic, and decorate with truffles. Then have ready a nice lobster butter, and shape it high. Put it in the mould, on the aspic, and pour aspic jelly round. When cold turn out, and garnish with hard-boiled eggs and truffles.

Fillets of Beef, with Mushrooms.

INGREDIENTS :

Fillets of beef.
Mushrooms.

Onion.
Spinach.

Have a few nice round fillets of beef, cut rather thick. Cook them nicely, and dish up on rounds of toast. Place mushrooms on the top of each fillet, rubbing first the fillets in onion. Serve with a very thick gravy, and spinach in centre of dish.

How to serve Prawns for Lunch.

INGREDIENTS:

Large lemon.
Prawns.
Bread-and-butter.

Parsley.
Lemon-juice.

Cut a nice large lemon in half, lengthways, and begin by sticking in a prawn from the centre of the lemon, and continue sticking in the prawns (by the sharp points in their heads) in circles, until the lemon is entirely covered. Ornament with parsley, and serve round them rolls of thin bread-and-butter, which has had a few drops of lemon-juice squeezed on it before rolling up.

Kidney Toast.

INGREDIENTS:

Ox kidney.
Onion.

Brown gravy.
Sherry.

Take some ox kidney, cut it up small, and flour it well. Then fry it in a stewpan, with some onion, until brown, and then add half a tablespoonful of brown gravy, pepper and salt. Simmer for about ten minutes. Then thicken with a little flour, add some sherry, and a little lemon juice at the last. Serve on rounds of toast, with stuffed tomatoes round.

Savoury Hashed Mutton.

INGREDIENTS:

Mutton.
Onions.
Tarragon vinegar.

Worcester sauce.
Red-currant jelly.

Fry nice and brown some sliced onions, then pour in any stock that you may have, and a little tarragon vinegar and Worcester sauce, and a spoonful of red-currant jelly. Simmer all together well; add a little flour, previously mixed with a spoonful of the stock: that will thicken the sauce. Rub it through a tammy, and then put it into a clean saucepan, and lay in the slices of cold mutton. Let all get quite hot, gently so as not to harden the meat. Mind the sauce is of a quite dark brown colour. Serve in a silver dish, with fried sippets of bread, and a bunch of fried parsley on the top.

Marrow Moulds.

INGREDIENTS:

Small vegetable marrows.
Fried rounds of bread.

Nicely made mince.
Curry gravy.

Take some small marrows, and boil them whole. When cooked, cut in half carefully, and take out a little of the inside, so as to form a cup. Fill up with nicely made mince (hot), and put each marrow cup on the fried bread. Serve with a brown curry sauce.

Cutlets à la Diable.

INGREDIENTS:

Cutlets.
Breadcrumbs.
Egg.

Lard (or dripping).
Tomato sauce.

Have some very nice, thick mutton cutlets, season with pepper, salt, mustard, and a little onion rubbed over them. Then egg and breadcrumb, and fry in boiling lard or butter.

Dish up with cutlet-frills on each, and serve very hot, with a good tomato sauce, and fried potato chips, cut very thin, in centre of the dish.

Braised Lamb Cutlets, au purée de Marrow.

INGREDIENTS:

Lamb cutlets.
Braised sauce.

Chestnuts.

Cut some very neat lamb cutlets, remove all the fat, and trim them. Steam them until tender, about ten minutes, then make a very nice braised sauce. Arrange the cutlets on a *purée* of chestnuts. Pour over and entirely cover each cutlet with sauce, and the bottom of the dish. Make all very hot, and put a small frill round each cutlet bone.

Salines of Chicken or Partridge.

INGREDIENTS:

Game or poultry.	Truffles.
Bread.	Tomatoes.
Mushrooms.	Butter.

Have ready a few nice pieces of poultry or game, and arrange as hot, round piece of fried bread, at the bottom of a silver dish. Stand a tall piece of hot fried bread in the centre. Spread a skewer with cooked mushrooms and truffles, and stick it into the tall piece of bread. Grill the pieces of poultry or chicken nicely in butter, then arrange them neatly on the round piece of bread; then pour round and over a very nice, thick brown gravy or sauce. Garnish with tomatoes, and serve very hot.

Kidneys in Bacon.

INGREDIENTS:

Sheep's kidneys.	Bacon.
Pepper.	

Cut some fresh sheep's kidneys in half, and pepper them well. Next wrap each half kidney up in a nice slice of bacon, and skewer them with tiny game skewers. Fry quickly over a very hot fire for ten minutes. Then dish up in a hot silver dish, first removing the skewer. (This is also very nice for breakfast.)

How to Cook Sweetbreads.

First soak or blanch the sweetbreads in luke-warm water (that has a little vinegar in it), for about two hours; then put into boiling water, and cook until tender, but firm. Take them out, and put into cold water, until quite cold; then they are ready for use. If for frying, egg-and-breadcrumb them, and fry either in slices or whole, and serve nicely. Serve a nice, piquant sauce with them; or if to be served white, boil them for a few minutes. Mind and put them into boiling water, and serve a thick white sauce over, and mushrooms. Sprinkle a little chopped parsley over to make it look nice. Of course there are a great many different dishes made from sweetbreads, such as *vol-au-vents*, &c.

Sweetbread Soufflé.

INGREDIENTS :

4 ozs. butter.
4 ozs. flour.
1 pint milk.
Cayenne pepper and salt.
3 ozs. chopped mushrooms
3 ozs. chopped tongue.
1 large sweetbread.
4 eggs.

Melt the butter, and stir in the flour and milk, a little pepper and salt, juice of a lemon, and then the mushrooms and chopped tongue, and the sweetbread chopped very fine, that has been previously blanched and cooked until tender. Stir all this over the fire, until it boils. Then turn it into a basin, and when cold mix in the yolks of the four eggs. Beat the whites to a stiff froth, and add last. Put all into a fireproof or silver soufflé dish, and bake in a quick oven, about twenty minutes.

Sweetbread Fritters à la Claudine.

INGREDIENTS:

Sweetbread, blanched and cooked.
Lemon-juice.

Pepper and salt.
Batter (Recipe No. 5).
Hot fat.

Cut the sweetbread into pieces about half an inch thick and the size of a five-shilling piece. Sprinkle each slice with lemon-juice, and pepper and salt. Dip in a batter, and fry in hot fat for about ten minutes. Drain carefully and dish up on a round silver dish, one fritter overlapping the other, and fill up the centre with green peas.

Kidney Slices.

INGREDIENTS:

2 sheep's kidneys.
1 calf's kidney.
Onion.
Parsley.

Pepper and salt.
Breadcrumbs.
Egg.

Take two sheep's and one calf's kidney with the fat on. Bake them, and when done chop up very fine with a little onion, parsley, pepper and salt. Then cut some rounds of bread, egg-and-breadcrumb them, and fry in butter, placing the kidney on the top. Serve very hot, and decorate with fried slices of tomatoes—that is, put a slice of tomato between each kidney.

Little Tit-Bits.

Ingredients:

Round of fried bread. | Mince of either game, fowl,
Hard-boiled eggs. | or meat.

Take some rounds of bread and fry a golden brown. Have ready a little mince of any remains of cold meat, or fowl, or game, hot and nicely flavoured with stock, sauces, onions, &c. Put a lump of the mince on each piece of bread, and decorate with hard-boiled egg, and serve.

Cutlets à la Milanaise.

Ingredients:

Veal cutlets. | Macaroni.
Butter. | Tomato sauce.
Shallots. |

Fry the veal cutlets in a stewpan with a little butter, also the shallots chopped, until a nice brown colour. Then draw the pan to the side of the fire, and let the cutlets stew very slowly for half an hour. Then add two tablespoonfuls of tomato sauce, and simmer slowly for a quarter of an hour. Have boiled in another pan some nice lengths of macaroni, and dish the cutlets up in a silver dish, with the macaroni piled high in the centre.

Chicken Croquettes.

INGREDIENTS:

2 ozs. butter.	¼ lb. minced chicken and tongue.
2 eggs.	Worcester sauce.
1 dessertspoonful of flour.	
Salt and pepper.	

Beat the butter to a cream, add to it slowly the eggs, flour, salt, pepper, &c., and lastly mix in the chicken and tongue and flour, with a little Worcester sauce. Leave until wanted on a plate to set. Form into little balls about the size of a golf ball. Egg-and-breadcrumb carefully, and fry in boiling lard in a frying basket. Dish up on a border of mashed potato, made in a circle, round a silver dish, and fill up the centre with a nice *purée* of spinach, or green peas whole.

Egg Kromiskies.

INGREDIENTS:

Eggs (as many as required). | Batter for frying.

Boil the eggs for three minutes and peel carefully, and dip each into frying batter, and fry in boiling lard for one minute only. Dish up with little rolls of fried hot bacon.

Curried Eggs.

INGREDIENTS:

3 onions sliced	1 pint stock
1 oz. butter	4 hard-boiled eggs.
1 teaspoonful curry-paste.	1 gill of cream.
1 teaspoonful curry-powder.	

Fry the onions in the butter and a little flour,

then when brown add the curry-paste and powder, and the stock, and two lumps of sugar. Let all stew until the onions are quite tender, then add the cream and simmer for three or four minutes. Next strain the sauce through a fine sieve, and lay the hard-boiled eggs in it, first having cut them in slices or quarters. Let all get quite hot, but do not let them boil. Dish up in centre of silver dish, with border of nicely boiled rice.

Mushrooms à la Margaretta.

INGREDIENTS:

Mushrooms.	Pepper and salt.
Butter.	Bacon.

Take as many little china fireproof ramequin cases as required, allowing one for each person. Cut up some fresh field button mushrooms, not too small, and fill each case alternately with fresh butter, pepper, salt, and mushrooms. On the top place a round of fat, uncooked bacon. Place the china cases in a baking tin full of water (be careful the water does not get in the cases), and allow them to poach rather slowly in a brisk oven. Dish up on a clean folded napkin, and garnish each with a piece of parsley. This is very good, either as an *entrée* or breakfast dish. A great improvement is to add a little lemon-juice.

Larded Oysters on Mushrooms.

INGREDIENTS :

Mushrooms.
Lemon-juice.
Oysters.

Batter (Recipe No. 5).
Larding bacon.

Beard the oysters and lard each one twice with lardoons about an inch long, and not very thick. Have ready a very nice frying batter, and mask each oyster in it. Fry quickly in boiling fat until a nice golden colour. Dish up each oyster when cooked on a hot fried mushroom, which has been well flavoured with lemon-juice and well peppered. Dish the mushroom, with the oyster on it, on a nicely fried *croûton* of bread, in a circle, in a silver dish, round hot rolled little slices of bacon. Serve very hot.

Œufs à la Tongue (for Breakfast or Lunch).

INGREDIENTS :

Eggs.
Kidneys.

Parsley.
Butter.

Poach as many eggs as are required all together in the oven, and have some kidneys nicely stewed. Place the kidneys in the centre of the dish, and the eggs round the edge of the dish. Sprinkle chopped parsley over. Serve very hot.

IV
JOINTS AND SIDE DISHES

(WRINKLE)

During "fly" season the plates should be turned bottom side up.

Rolled Spiced Beef.

INGREDIENTS :

6 lbs. of flank of beef.
1 oz. of bay salt.
1 oz. of common salt.
Blade of mace.

Allspice.
Cloves.
Pepper.

ORDER a piece of the long flank of beef, fresh, about 5 or 6 lbs. Take out any little bones there may be, and any pieces of skin on the inside of it (not the outside). Lay it out flat on a dish, then pound the bay salt and common salt together, also pound the mace, a few allspice, cloves, and some pepper all together, and add them to the salt. Carefully rub the inside and outside with this mixture, using it all. Let the beef lie in it for twenty-four hours, then roll it round carefully and tie with tape, and put it into a brawn tin or cake mould. Tie it down carefully, and put into a saucepan of boiling water, and let it boil until the beef is done. Take care that the water does not get into the tin. When the beef has been cooking for an hour or so, just take the lid off and press down the beef, either with a saucer or anything you like, and put it on again; it will then take from four to six hours' boiling. You can tell when it is done by trying it with a fork. Let it get cold in the tin, and then turn it out. This is most delicious either winter or summer. Another way to cook it is to put the tin in the potato steamer, and have the boiling water in the saucepan, only it must be kept full, so that there is plenty of steam to cook it.

Rolled Loin of Mutton, stuffed with Apple Sauce.

INGREDIENTS :

| Loin of Mutton. | Chives |
| Apples. | Breadcrumbs. |

Have a loin of mutton boned (put the bones down for a good stock), and before rolling it up to roast spread on the inside a stuffing made of apples and onions chopped fine, and a few breadcrumbs. Roll up and skewer, and roast in a hot oven, nice and brown. Serve with red-currant jelly or apple sauce.

Boiled Leg of Mutton.

INGREDIENTS :

Leg of mutton.	Onions.
Carrots.	Capers.
Turnips.	Spices.
Sugar.	

Wrap the leg up in a floured cloth, and put into a saucepan of boiling water. Add nicely cut carrots, turnips, and onions, two lumps of sugar, and a few spices. Let it all boil up once, then draw it to the side of the fire, and let it simmer gently until done. Time, twenty minutes to every pound. Dish up carefully, and pour a little rich caper sauce over, and garnish with the vegetables. Serve some sauce in a sauce-boat.

How to make three small Joints out of a Sirloin of Beef.

1st Joint.—Take out the fillet, or undercut, and lard it. Roast or braise it, and serve it with horse-radish sauce and tomatoes.

2nd Joint.—Roast the top of the sirloin, and serve Yorkshire pudding with it, and scraped horse-radish.

3rd Joint.—Stew carefully, with vegetables, the tail or end of the sirloin, and serve very hot, with a thick gravy.

Pressed Beef. (*Cold.*)

INGREDIENTS :

10 lbs. of spiced brisket of beef.	Carrot.
Onion.	Herbs.
	Glaze.

Put the beef into a saucepan of warm water, not hot, and add an onion, carrot, bay-leaf, chives, and a little sugar. Let it come gently to the boil, then draw it off on one side and allow it to simmer until tender and inclined to leave the bones. Take the pan off the fire, and take away the short bones; put it back, and leave for half an hour in the liquor in which it was boiled. Take it up, and press between two flat dishes; put between the linen-press and screw down. Leave until the next day, then trim all the edges and glaze it over. If you have no linen-press put weights on the top of the dish. This is very nice for lunches in the hot weather.

Rolled Stuffed Steak.

INGREDIENTS :

| Beef-steak. | Breadcrumbs. |
| Horseradish. | Egg. |

Take about 2 lbs. of beef-steak, lay it on a chopping board, and beat it with a rolling pin for quite ten minutes, then place the following stuffing on the steak, tie up very tightly with tape. Put it in a hot oven, with a piece of well-buttered paper over it, and a little dripping in the pan ; baste for twenty minutes. When done take it up, and serve with horseradish sauce, or scraped horseradish on top, and some parsley. Pour the gravy round which comes from the steak.

Stuffing for Steak.—Mix a handful of freshly made breadcrumbs, a tablespoonful of chopped chives, 1 oz. of butter, pepper and salt, and mix with a well-beaten egg.

Fillet of Beef (Larded).

INGREDIENTS :

| Fillet of beef. | Vegetables. |
| Bacon for larding. | |

Lard a nice fillet of beef, cook it carefully, and when done arrange round it, in separate bunches, French beans, peas, carrot balls, potato balls, cauliflower, or shallots. Then pour over the fillet a nice thick brown sauce.

Stuffed Boned Neck of Lamb.

INGREDIENTS :

Neck of lamb.
Breadcrumbs.
Egg.

Chopped tongue.
Truffles.
Bacon.

Stuff a neck of lamb with a nice savoury forcemeat made of breadcrumbs, yolk of egg, salt, chopped tongue, bacon, truffles. Then roll round, and roast until done. Serve very hot, with a nice brown sauce poured over.

Collared Head or Brawn.

INGREDIENTS :

Pig's head and tongue.
Spice.

Pepper.

Put a pig's head and tongue into salt for three or four days. Wash it thoroughly, and boil it for about three hours and a half. Cut the tongue into rather large pieces, and mince the rest quite fine, mixing fat and lean as equally as possible. Be very careful to cut out any black speck or skin. Heat the tin and the plates you cut on, and do it as quickly as possible, that the fat may run out before it is cold. Mix about a teaspoonful of spice with each plateful. Have the following spices ground ready : black and white pepper, allspice, cloves. Put a heavy weight on it, and let it stand until next day.

How to Boil Pork.

Lay the pork in cold water, and allow quarter of an hour to each pound after the water boils, and mind and put about two heaped dessertspoonfuls of brown sugar with the water.

A Nice Way of Doing up Cold Meat, à la Toodles.

INGREDIENTS :

Remains of cold meat.	Tomatoes.
Herbs.	Mushrooms.
Pepper and salt.	Oiled butter.
Breadcrumbs.	Harvey sauce.

Chop up any cold meat, and season with chopped herbs, pepper, salt, and Harvey sauce. Strew some breadcrumbs into a well-greased pie-dish, and put alternately layers of chopped meat and sliced tomatoes or mushrooms, until the dish is full, then sprinkle thickly with breadcrumbs, and pour a little oiled butter over. Bake in a very good oven, and brown well. Serve in the same dish.

Good Breakfast Dish.

INGREDIENTS :

Sausage meat.	Egg.
Mashed potato.	Breadcrumbs.

Take the sausage meat and make into balls. Cover each with nicely flavoured mashed potato. Egg and breadcrumb, and fry in boiling fat until a nice golden colour. Serve very hot. Little rolls of fried bacon can be served with this.

Pope Patties.

INGREDIENTS :

Short crust.
4 hard-boiled eggs.
12 fresh mushrooms.

Pepper and salt.
Oiled butter.

Line some patty-pans with short crust, and fill each with the following mixture : hard-boiled eggs and mushrooms, flavoured with pepper, salt, chopped very fine ; then pour a little oiled butter on each, and cover with paste. Bake in a quick oven, and serve very hot.

Beef and Rice.

INGREDIENTS :

2 lbs. lean beef.
Carrot, turnip, onion, celery, and parsley (all chopped up fine).

Pepper and salt.
Rice.
Butter.
Curry-powder.

Take the beef—slices from a rolled rib do best—and stew it in a little water with the vegetables until tender. Season with pepper and salt. The vegetables should be boiled to a pulp, and the gravy very rich and thick. Boil some rice in slightly salted water. When it is done, and quite dry, add to it a lump of butter and some curry-powder. Put the beef on the dish with the rice round, and serve very hot.

Boned Roast Pigeons.

INGREDIENTS:

| Pigeons. | Stuffing. |
| Butter. | Bacon. |

Take four nice young pigeons and bone them carefully. Have a stuffing ready made like the following, and when you have stuffed them nicely, truss and tie them up in a piece of fat bacon, and place each on a piece of toast. Roast them in front of a clear, bright fire for fifteen minutes, basting them with butter all the time. When done, take off the bacon, and pour over them a dark brown glazed sauce, and serve each on the piece of toast they were roasted on, with fried breadcrumbs round them. Serve bread sauce with them.

Stuffing for Pigeons or Chickens.—Take a large handful of fresh breadcrumbs, the same of chopped bacon and tongue, if you have any, a lump of butter, pepper and salt, and a little lemon-juice, and finely chopped onion or chives. Bind together with an egg, and make all into a smooth paste. It is then ready for use, and very delicious.

Pigeon Pudding.

INGREDIENTS:

Pigeons.	Pepper and salt.
Lemon-juice.	Beef-steak.
Onion.	

Prepare some pigeons as if for some pigeon pie, season each piece with cayenne pepper, lemon-juice, onion, and salt. Line a pudding basin with very nice rich suet crust, put in the pigeons, with 1 lb. of good beef-steak. Fill up the basin with a nicely flavoured stock, and cover over with the crust. Tie up in a floured cloth, and boil for two and a half hours. Remove the cloth, and serve the pudding in the basin with a clean napkin tied round it. An orange salad served with this is a great improvement.

Boiled Chicken.

Ingredients :

| Chicken. | Onion. |
| Salt. | Sugar. |

Truss the chicken for boiling, and see it is a nice shape. Wrap it up in a well-buttered paper, and then in a floured cloth. Have ready a saucepan (large enough to hold the chicken easily) of boiling water, in which has been boiled a sliced onion, a few lumps of sugar, and salt. Put in the chicken, and let it come to the boil quickly, then draw the saucepan on one side and let it simmer gently for twenty minutes. Take up and remove the cloth and paper and pour over a thick, hot, white Béchamel sauce, and sprinkle finely chopped parsley over. Decorate round the chicken with little rolls of fried bacon and little bunches of already-cooked vegetable, such as nicely cut carrots and turnips. If the chicken is to be served cold, pour the white sauce over, when the chicken is cold, and see that it is entirely covered. Leave it to set, then put the chicken carefully on a clean dish, and decorate with the yolk of a hard-boiled egg put through a fine sieve, and decorate the dish with finely cut beetroot and fresh parsley.

How to Roast an Old Fowl.

INGREDIENTS :

Fowl.
Bacon.

Bread sauce.

First truss it nicely, and then boil for twenty minutes slowly. Take it up and roast in a hot oven for three-quarters of an hour. Serve with bread sauce and rolls of fried bacon. Cooked like this the fowl is like a young chicken.

Mutton a la Paine.

INGREDIENTS :

Cold mutton.
Chives or onions.
Red-currant jelly.
Stock.

Worcester sauce.
Spinach (prepared).
Eggs.
Butter.

Mince up finely some cold mutton, also a little onion or chives; add Marshall's coraline pepper, Worcester sauce, and salt to taste. Put into a basin, and moisten with a little nice stock, a little red-currant jelly, and Worcester sauce. Do not make the mixture too moist, but nicely flavoured and hot. Take some little white china fireproof dishes and butter them. Put at the bottom a layer of nicely prepared spinach *purée;* then put in a layer of the hot mutton, and on the top break a fresh egg; place a little piece of butter on the top. Fill as many dishes as required and put them to poach in a deep pan of water in a quick oven until the eggs are quite set. Arrange prettily on a folded napkin, and garnish each with finely chopped parsley. Serve very hot as an *entrée* or breakfast dish.

Devilled Mutton Slices.

INGREDIENTS :

Cold mutton.
Onion.

Chili vinegar.
Brown sugar.

Cut as many slices of mutton as you require rather thick, and lay them, made hot, in a little mushroom ketchup, Worcester sauce, a little chopped onion, and chili or tarragon vinegar, and a little brown sugar—all mixed together to liking. Put all into a fireproof dish, or if preferred an enamel pan, with a buttered paper over, and put into the oven for fifteen minutes. Take up each slice and arrange them round a dish, one piece overlapping another, and pour a little of the mixture over them. Fill up the centre of the dish with hot green peas (bottled, if not fresh), and pour over the peas a little oiled butter with a little caster sugar in it. Serve all very hot. A little tomato butter on each slice of mutton is a great improvement to the taste and look of this dish.

Mutton Balls.

INGREDIENTS:

Cold mutton.
Allspice.
Pepper and salt.
Worcester sauce.

1 egg.
Mashed potato.
Breadcrumbs.
Green peas.

Pound up in the mortar some cold mutton very smooth, add some allspice, pepper and salt to taste, a little Worcester sauce, and bind with an egg. Put on a plate to set, and when cold form into balls. Have ready some mashed potatoes, mixed with salt and an egg to a smooth paste. Place a ball of the mutton on to a piece of potato, entirely covering it all, forming it into a ball not very large. Egg-and-breadcrumb and fry a golden brown in boiling fat. Dish up in a silver dish with a wall of green peas or beans round. Serve all very hot.

How to use up Cold Mutton.

Shred Mutton.

INGREDIENTS:

Cold mutton.
Onion.

Red-currant jelly.

Cut up an onion very small, add a sprinkling of flour to it and a small piece of butter. Put it into an enamel stewpan and let it all brown together. Then add a small pot of red-currant or gooseberry jelly, a cupful of any stock or gravy you have, Marshall's coraline pepper, and salt to taste; add a little chili vinegar. When all is quite hot and thoroughly mixed stir into it a small plateful (more if required) of cold mutton which has been previously cut into long, thin strips about two inches long and not too thick. Let all get thoroughly covered with the gravy, which should be thick enough to stick to the mutton like a curry. Turn out and pile high in the centre of a silver dish, and garnish round with slices of devilled tomato and a bunch of hot fried parsley on the top of the mutton. This is delicious.

V

VEGETABLES AND SALADS

(WRINKLES)

In boiling greens of any kind put them in boiling water with plenty of room. Add a lump of sugar, put half a thick slice of bread on the top of the water, boil without a lid, and there will be no disagreeable smell; the colour will also be preserved.

In cooking peas use sugar in the water instead of salt, and cook spinach without water.

How to Cook Carrots and Turnips for serving with Cutlets and Steaks.

CUT up into narrow, short pieces the carrots and turnips. Wash them well and drain off the water. Put them into an enamel saucepan with a lump of butter, salt, and pepper. Let them cook slowly until quite tender, and arrange in centre of dish for cutlets. Vegetables cooked in this way are delicious in clear soups.

French Beans, boiled whole.

Cut the ends off the French beans or scarlet runners, put them into boiling water with a little salt, and boil with the lid off until quite tender. Drain them carefully, add a lump of fresh butter, and serve very hot.

Vegetable Marrow (How to Cook).

Just wash the marrow carefully, and on no account cut or scrape it. Put into boiling water and remove when tender. Drain, and serve with nicely made white sauce.

Potato Balls.

Mash some cooked potatoes in a mortar and mix with 1½ ozs. of butter, pepper and salt, and chopped parsley. Make up into small lumps, brush over with oiled butter, and bake in the oven a nice brown.

Haricot Beans.

INGREDIENTS:

| Haricot beans. | Butter. |
| Water. | Sugar. |

Put as many beans as required to soak in cold water for eight or nine hours; then boil carefully with a little sugar in the water. When quite tender drain, and serve with a lump of fresh butter on them.

Haricot Purée.

INGREDIENTS:

Haricot beans.	Sugar.
Water.	Cream.
Butter.	Pepper and salt.

Boil until tender, after having soaked them as in preceding recipe. Press while hot through a fine hair sieve. Mix in a lump of fresh butter, pepper and salt, and a gill of cream. Mix altogether, and put into a basin and steam. Turn out carefully, and serve.

Asparagus.

Wash the asparagus and tie into small bundles with tape, and lay them in cold water until to be cooked. Then stand all the bundles up in a deep saucepan over the potato steamer, and let them steam until tender. Dish up on a slice of hot toast, and serve oiled butter with a little drop of lemon-juice in it.

Beetroot. (*Hot.*)

Boil some nice young beetroots, and when cold cut into thin slices. Have ready a nice white sauce well flavoured with fried onions, and when the sauce is hot put in the beetroot slices and boil two or three minutes. Dish up in centre of a silver dish, and put a wall of nicely mashed potato round.

Spinach.

This is best steamed, as it is so full of moisture. When tender press through a wire sieve, and add a lump of butter and a gill of cream. Put back to get quite hot. Serve very hot with fried *croûtons* round.

Young Early Carrots.

Boil until quite tender in butter. When done dish up and sprinkle finely chopped parsley over. Serve with plenty of fresh oiled butter in the dish.

How to Cook Mushrooms.

Peel them carefully and arrange bottom upwards, not one on top of each other, in a Yorkshire pudding tin or large, flat, enamel stewpan (the latter preferred, as it is best to have a lid on, as the steam keeps the flavour in and makes the mushrooms tender). Place a small lump of butter on each mushroom, with plenty of pepper and salt and about a tablespoonful of water. Put them over a clear, bright fire, and let them simmer slowly until tender (they take about twenty minutes), and when done take up carefully and arrange on little rounds of toast, or in a heap in the centre of the dish. Of course, it depends upon what they are required for.

To Keep French Beans and Scarlet Runners for Winter Use.

Pick the beans when dry and put them into a large earthenware pan, with plenty of common salt between each layer. Press down tight; don't cut the beans up. Keep them quite air-tight by putting a bladder over each jar. When the beans are wanted lay them in cold water for two hours, and then cut up and boil like fresh beans.

Potato Croquettes.

INGREDIENTS:

1 oz. fresh butter.
2 eggs.
1 dessertspoonful of flour.

1 saltspoonful of salt.
½ lb. potatoes boiled and grated.

Beat the butter to a cream, add to it slowly the eggs, flour, salt, and the potatoes. Mix well into a smooth paste, and form into lengths of about two inches long and one inch round. Egg-and-bread-crumb carefully, and fry in hot lard or clarified dripping, and serve very hot, with a bunch of fried parsley in the centre.

Potato Scallops.

INGREDIENTS:

1 lb. nice potatoes (boiled).   1 oz. butter.
¼ pint cream.   Pepper and salt.

Mash up the potatoes very finely in the mortar, with the cream, butter, pepper, and salt. When quite mixed put some into little white china scallop-shells, with a little bit of butter on the top. Put them into the oven in a pan of water. Let them poach until hot. Sprinkle over each some finely chopped parsley, and serve. Instead of the parsley the stiffly whipped white of an egg, like meringues, looks very pretty, and just left in the oven to brown, and then sprinkle over the parsley.

Baked Tomatoes.

Take some ripe English tomatoes, and cut off about half an inch at the top. Place a lump of bread-crumbs and butter where you cut off the top, and put all into a baking pan, and bake for half an hour. Serve them with the juice that comes from them.

How to Cook New Potatoes.

Wash and brush them, not scrape. Then put them into boiling water, and boil until tender. Dish up carefully, and pour oiled butter, with finely chopped parsley, over them.

Old potatoes ought never to be put into water; they should be boiled in a steamer in their skins, and when done take off the steamer and put a clean napkin on the potatoes to absorb any water caused by the steam. When sent to table they should be perfectly dry, and floury when peeled.

Potatoes for Breakfast.

Cut up any cold potatoes you may have, and after having fried the bacon for breakfast put the slices of potatoes in the bacon pan, and fry a nice golden colour in the fat left from the bacon. Dish up high in the centre of a silver dish, and arrange the rashers of bacon nicely round. Serve very hot.

Baked Potatoes.

Pick out large-sized potatoes, wash and scrub the skins quite clean, then put to bake in a hot oven until tender. Dish up in a nicely folded fish napkin, and hand little pats of butter with them and a jug of cream; then just pull the potato open, and put a pat of butter and a little cream in each. These are most delicious with cold meats.

Orange Salad for Wild Duck.

Peel and scrape off the orange every bit of white skin, then divide into separate pieces, and arrange high in a salad plate. Pour over a teaspoonful of salad oil and one of chili vinegar, and sprinkle a little white sugar over.

Lobster Salad à la Maude.

Make a rich mayonnaise sauce, and then get all the meat out of a lobster and the cream from the head; cut it up very fine and mix with the sauce, and flavour well with anchovy sauce and pepper. Have some lettuces and endive quite dry and crisp, and pull into pieces, arranging them round the salad bowl high like a wall. Then pour in the lobster and sauce, and lastly put the meat from the claws, cut in large pieces, on the top of the sauce. Garnish with hard-boiled eggs and the coral from the lobster, put through a sieve, and stand up in the centre of all the two feelers of the lobster.

Cucumber and Tomato Salad (*very pretty and delicious*).

Take some fresh English tomatoes and cut into slices; arrange them round the bottom of a soup-plate like a wall, next place a layer of nicely cut cucumber, and after that another layer of tomatoes. Fill up the centre of the wall with the following dressing: Mix in a basin three tablespoonfuls of best salad oil and a teaspoonful of brown sugar, mix thoroughly, and then add two tablespoonfuls of chili vinegar and one of tarragon; lastly put in a small handful of finely cut-up chives, and use for the salad.

Beetroot and Celery Salad.

Cut some beetroot into thin round slices, and form a wall of them round the bottom of a soup-plate.

Fill up the centre with square-cut pieces of celery; fill it up nice and high. Pour over a salad dressing (recipe given), and just before serving scrape a little horseradish very finely on the top of the celery.

Very Good Salad Dressing. (*A Favourite.*)

Put into a basin the yolk of a fresh egg. Add to it a little raw mustard, caster sugar, and salt and pepper. Stir slowly with a wooden spoon, and gradually work in the best salad oil to the quantity of two tablespoonfuls; then add a tablespoonful of chili vinegar and one of tarragon vinegar, and a little cream if you have any. Just at the last scrape in the heart of an onion or a few finely chopped chives.

French Salad Dressing.

Mix a little salt and pepper in a large tablespoonful of oil, and let the salt dissolve. Then add about three more tablespoonfuls of oil, and when well mixed add a tablespoonful of tarragon and one of chili vinegar.

My Salad.

Take the best and hardest-hearted French lettuces and same of endive. Pull off the outer leaves, and put the rest as they are into a basin of strong cold salted water, and leave until required. Then take out, and pump over them fresh cold water, and leave them to drain on a hair sieve. Pull each leaf off carefully, and lay in a cloth to dry; do not cut the leaves. Finish all in this way, and arrange the lettuces in the centre of a soup-plate or salad-bowl, and arrange the endive round the edge. Put washed chives in small bunches out of centre of salad, and hand the salad dressing given on page 80. Hard-boiled egg, cut in fancy slices, can be used to decorate the salad if liked, or beetroot.

Shrimp or Prawn Salad.

This is a very nice salad, made exactly like the lobster salad, only using shrimps or prawns instead of lobster. It can be decorated and arranged in precisely the same way as the lobster salad.

French Bean Salad.

Boil the beans whole, and when done leave to get cold. Then cut in halves, and pile up high in dish, and pour a nicely made mayonnaise sauce over all, or salad dressing (Recipe on page 80).

Mushrooms as a Vegetable.

INGREDIENTS:

Mushrooms (field ones if in season).
¼ lb. butter.

Pepper and salt.
Tablespoonful of water, not more.

Put the mushrooms, after having peeled and cut off the stalks carefully, into a vegetable dish with the butter, pepper and salt, and water. Then put the cover on the dish, and put it in the oven, and let them cook slowly for one hour. Shake the dish occasionally, and baste them. Serve in the same dish, and send in as a vegetable.

Stuffed Tomatoes.

Ingredients:

Tomatoes (all the same size if possible).
Chicken liver.
Pepper and salt.
Butter.
Breadcrumbs.

Take nice fresh, ripe tomatoes, cut off the tops, scrape out all the inside, and fill up with the following mixture, and bake on a buttered tin. Serve each one on a fried *croûton* of bread, and serve very hot in a silver dish, with a little white of egg whipped to a stiff froth on each.

Mixture.—Pound the chicken liver with pepper, salt, and butter; then mix in the tomato pulp. Mix well, and fill each tomato-case full, and sprinkle breadcrumbs on top.

VI
PUDDINGS AND SWEETS

Pear Meringue.

INGREDIENTS :

Pears.
Sugar.
Water.

Marshall's carmine.
Custard.

Stew some pears nicely, first peeling and cutting them in half lengthways, and coreing them. Put them into a stewpan, with very little water but plenty of sugar. Simmer until tender. Then add a few drops of Marshall's carmine to make a good colour. When done, take them out and leave them in their syrup to get cold. While they are cooling, make a nice custard, and place the pears in a cut-glass dish, and then pour the custard when cold on the pears gently, so as not to mix it with the fruit. Next whip up the whites of the eggs (that you have over from making the custard) with caster sugar until stiff, and put roughly on the top of the custard like meringue, and sprinkle chopped pistachio nuts over (cold sweet).

Short-crust for Cakes or Tarts.

INGREDIENTS :

1 lb. of flour.
6 ozs. of butter.

1 egg.
2 ozs. of powdered sugar.

Rub the butter in the flour, then the sugar and the

yolk of the egg. Add a little water and make a stiff paste. Roll out and use.

Sayer's Plum-pudding.

Ingredients:

1 lb. best raisins.
1 lb. currants.
1 lb. sugar.
½ lb. sultanas.
½ lb mixed peel.
¼ lb. chopped almonds
¼ lb. flour.
½ lb. breadcrumbs.

1 lb. kidney beef suet.
6 or 8 eggs.
Milk if wanted (a glassful of brandy will be better than the milk).
Rind of 1 lemon chopped.
½ teaspoonful of salt.
1 teaspoonful of mixed spice.

Grease some pudding basins, and have ready string, pudding cloths, and greased white paper. Prepare the fruit, shred the peel, blanch and chop the almonds, make the breadcrumbs, chop the suet finely, and mix all the dry ingredients first. Break the eggs and beat the yolks and whites separately and thoroughly. Add the eggs, brandy, and milk, and mix all well.

Puff Pastry.

Ingredients:

1 lb. of Vienna flour.
1 lb. of fresh butter.
Pinch of salt.

Juice of 1 lemon.
Yolk of 1 large or 2 small eggs.

Put the flour and salt into a basin. Beat up the yolk of egg and lemon-juice with ¾ of a pint of cold water; pour this into a hole made in the middle of the flour, and mix well into a dough with a knife. Flour the board, and roll the dough into the size of a dinner plate. Put the butter into a clean cloth to squeeze out all the buttermilk. Put this lump on the pastry, and fold up like an apple dumpling. Flour the top and leave for a few minutes. Then roll it out to a long straight piece about half a yard long and a quarter broad. Fold this in three and roll out, fold again and roll out, always the same way, from you. Flour a cold, clean baking-sheet, and put the pastry on, and leave it in a cool place for half an hour; put on board and fold in three, and roll again twice; put it in the cold for quarter of an hour; put on board, fold and roll twice, making in all seven times. Now it is ready for use for tartlets or mince-pies, roll the pastry to the thickness of a penny; but for patties and *vol-au-vents*, the pastry should have one more roll, making eight, and be rolled out to a quarter of an inch thickness. Bake in hot oven.

Baked Apple Pudding.

INGREDIENTS.

Suet crust.	Apples.
Butter.	Cloves.
Sugar.	Cream.

Make a rich suet crust, and butter and sugar a pudding basin well. Then line the basin with the suet crust, and fill up with sliced apples, a few cloves, and plenty of sugar. Cover over the top with more suet crust, and put it to bake on a tin in a nice hot oven. Before sending it to table turn out carefully, and serve Devonshire cream or fresh butter, and brown sugar with it. You can also make this pudding of plums, pears, rhubarb, or oranges.

Sponge Cake Castles.

INGREDIENTS.

Sponge cake mixture.	Cream.
Apricot jam.	Almonds.
Strawberry jam.	

Make a sponge cake mixture (like recipe for sponge cake), only pour the mixture into large flat tins. When baked cut into rounds, commencing with a large one and finishing off with a very small one. Pile these on top of each other, spreading between each apricot and strawberry jam. When you have piled the rounds up high in the dish you wish to serve it on, and the cake is cold, pour whipped cream over and stick blanched almonds in it, and sprinkle chopped pistachio nuts over all.

Golden Drops.

INGREDIENTS.

Rice.	Lemon-juice.
Brown sugar.	Milk.
Butter.	1 egg.

Put some rice in a pie-dish with the brown sugar and lump of butter. Fill up the pie-dish with milk and water, put it in the oven and leave until tender. When quite done, take up and put it into an enamel stewpan, and add some more milk and two tablespoonfuls of lemon-juice, and the egg well whipped, and let it simmer gently for twenty minutes, but not boil. Plenty of rice must be used, as it must be of the consistency of whipped cream. Pour the whole into a nice cut-glass or silver dish, and when cold place at equal distances spoonfuls of apricot, and on the top of the jam a spoonful of whipped cream.

Green Plum Tart.

INGREDIENTS.

| Green plums. | Short-crust. |
| Brown sugar. | |

Have any hard green plums picked that you may happen to have in your garden. Put them in a stew-pan and entirely cover with water (cold.) Let them cook gently until they are quite tender, and the skins just begin to crack. Pour away the water, and put them into the pie-dish that you are going to cook them in, with plenty of brown sugar. Cover over with short-crust, the recipe for which is given. Brush over with a little water, and sugar the top. Put in a hot oven, and let it cook for one hour. This is a most delicious tart, greatly improved with the addition of a little cream or custard.

Pears in Cream.

INGREDIENTS.

Cream.	Pears.
Sugar.	Red-currant jelly.
Vanilla.	

Take as many little glass tubs as required, and fill

with stiffly whipped cream flavoured with sugar and vanilla or Devonshire cream. Then drop in a whole cored pear which has been stewed in syrup only, and fill the centre of the pear where the core was taken from with red-currant jelly. Put a piece of Angelica sticking out of the jelly to form the stalk. Serve on fancy dish papers with little gold spoons to each.

Pear Charlotte. (*Hot.*)

INGREDIENTS.

Bread-and-butter. | Pears.
Sugar.

Line a round tin or copper mould, which has been well buttered and sugared, with nicely cut pieces of bread-and-butter ; entirely cover the mould to the top. Then have ready the pears, nicely stewed, with cloves, sugar, and two or three drops of Marshall's carmine to colour the pears. Then fill up the mould and place a piece of bread-and-butter on the top, and bake in a nice hot oven. When done, turn out carefully into a silver dish, and serve very hot with sugar sprinkled over it. Hand a jug of cream with it.

Rice and Pears.

INGREDIENTS.

Caramel. | Pears.
Almonds. | Rice.

Take some little plain dariole moulds, and line them all round and at the top with caramel. When set with about half an inch of caramel at the top, put in a small, stewed, hot, whole pear (cored), having first filled the hole with chopped sweet almonds. Then fill up the mould with stewed and well-flavoured rice, and leave all to get cold. Then turn out carefully, and serve in a row down a long narrow dish. Place whipped cream down each side of the dish, the cream being coloured down one side with Marshall's sap green. This sweet can be served either hot or cold ; if hot, use hot French custard in place of the cream.

Meringues.

INGREDIENTS :

Eggs. | Icing sugar.

Take two, three, or four eggs and put them on the scales in place of the weights. Take the weight of the eggs you wish to use in icing sugar which is finely powdered, ready for use. Break the eggs carefully and put the whites in a basin, and beat into a very stiff froth. Then stir in quickly the sugar, weighed out ; do not beat the sugar into the whites, only stir quickly. Place some of the meringue on to a waxed baking-tin with a dessert-spoon, shaped oval, sprinkle some sugar over, and bake in a very slow oven until a pale golden colour and the meringue is set.

Put between the cases whipped cream flavoured with vanilla.

Bread Pudding.

INGREDIENTS:

Stale bread. | Sugar.
Milk.

Take all the pieces of bread that are left in the bread-pan that are too small and too stale to use otherwise. Soak all in a basin of warm milk and water. Add sugar to taste. Place in a pie-dish a layer of jam, and then put the soaked bread and sugar on the top. Bake all in a nice hot oven, and brown the top nicely. This is a very nice pudding indeed. Currants or sultanas can be used instead of jam if preferred.

Apricots and Rice. (*Cold.*)

INGREDIENTS:

Jelly. | Rice (prepared like recipe
Apricots. | for rice mould).
Cream.

Line some dariole moulds with lemon or raspberry jelly—that is, pour into the mould a little warm jelly, about a quarter full; next place in the centre carefully half an apricot, and fill up the mould with hot, nicely flavoured, and well-cooked rice (the rice to be cooked as if for rice mould), and set the moulds on one side to get cold. When quite firm dip the moulds into hot water for a second or two, and turn out in a row down a long dish, or in a circle in a round silver dish. Put whipped cream on top of each mould, and little gold or silver spoons between each mould.

Prune Shape.

Ingredients.

½ a lb. of prunes or plums.
½ a pint of water.
½ an oz. of gelatine.
A little sugar.

Put into a stewpan the plums and water, and stew gently until the stones leave easily. While you are taking away the stones put the gelatine into the hot syrup to dissolve, adding a little sugar. Break the stones and put the kernels, blanched and chopped, to the prunes. Stir all together. Put into a border mould, and when set turn out and fill up the centre with whipped cream, and stick blanched and cut almonds out of the prune mould to look like a porcupine.

Petits château de trois couleurs.

Ingredients :

Red-currant jelly.
Chocolate cream.
Cream.
Vanilla.

Line a fancy border mould with red-currant jelly, and when it has set pour in cream flavoured with vanilla. When this has set fill up the mould with chocolate cream, and leave until cold. Turn out, and fill centre of mould with whipped cream. Hand wafers with it and serve cold.

Raspberries and Cream.

INGREDIENTS :

Raspberries. | Caster sugar.
Cream. |

Pick some fresh raspberries the day before they are wanted. Put them in a pie-dish with plenty of caster sugar. Take up the next day and half fill some little glasses or old china teacups (without handles) with the raspberries, and then fill up the glasses with nicely whipped cream. Sprinkle a little pink coffee sugar over the cream, and serve on a fancy dish-paper, with little gold spoons between each. If fruit is not in season, use nicely made jam in the same manner. If sponge fingers or vanilla wafers are handed with this sweet it is a great improvement.

Suet Pudding baked under the Meat.

INGREDIENTS :

½ a lb. of flour. | ¼ of a lb. of suet.

This mixture will make two puddings. Boil it for one hour on a plate, then put it under the meat for one hour, and baste well. Turn it when required.

Yorkshire Pudding.

INGREDIENTS :

4 tablespoonfuls of flour. | 3 eggs.
Milk. | Salt.

Put the flour and a pinch of salt into the basin,

and add sufficient milk to make a stiff batter. Add eggs, previously well beaten with the rest of the milk, to make a nice thin batter. Pour into a Yorkshire pudding tin, which has some hot dripping in it (the dripping from under the joint you are roasting is best, as you get the flavour from the meat). Put in a hot oven and bake about one and half hours. Cut into squares and serve.

French Plum-pudding.

INGREDIENTS :

6 ozs. of suet.
½ lb. of grated bread.
¼ lb. of sugar.
½ lb. of French plums.

3 well-beaten eggs.
1 small teacupful of milk.
1 dessertspoonful of brandy.
6 blanched almonds.

Mix all well together, let it stand for two hours, stir it well, and boil for four hours.

Baked Cream.

INGREDIENTS :

1 pint milk.
¼ lb. butter.
1 dessertspoonful of flour.
2 dessertspoonfuls of cornflour.

2 eggs.
1 oz. caster sugar.
Vanilla flavouring.

Put in an enamel stewpan nearly all the milk with the butter. Make a smooth batter with the rest of the milk and flour, and add it to the rest; let all boil for ten minutes. When cold beat into it the sugar and the yolks of eggs and vanilla flavouring. Beat the whites to a stiff froth and mix all together, and put into a buttered pie-dish. Put slices of blanched almonds, and bake in a quick oven for about half an hour.

Baked Plum-pudding.

INGREDIENTS :

½ lb. suet (finely chopped).
1 lb. flour.
Saltspoonful of salt.
1 oz. peel, mixed.
Teaspoonful of baking-powder.

½ lb. currants (washed, picked and dried).
1 oz. brown sugar.
2 eggs.

Mix all the dry ingredients with two eggs beaten up with as much milk as will make a thick batter. Pour all into a buttered pie-dish, and bake in a hot oven for about one and a half hours. Before serving turn the pudding out and sprinkle thickly with white sugar. Hand Devonshire cream with this pudding.

Dried Pippin Apples.

INGREDIENTS :

1 lb. equal to 6 lbs. of fresh apples.
1½ pints water.
1 dozen pippin apples.

Sugar.
Spice.
Lemon-rind.
Whipped cream.

Place the apples in an earthenware jar, add the cold water and let them soak nine or ten hours. Add sugar, spice, and the rind of a lemon to suit the taste. Then turn all into an enamel stewpan, and stew gently for one hour. When cold remove the cores and fill in with whipped cream, and serve.

Miniature Rice Moulds.

INGREDIENTS:

2 ozs. rice.
1 oz. butter.
½ pint milk.

¼ pint cream.
2 eggs.
1 oz. caster sugar.

Cook the rice in the milk until it is swollen and quite tender, then stir in the butter and let it cool. Then stir in the eggs, previously well beaten, and lastly add the cream and a little vanilla essence. Butter thoroughly some small dariole moulds, and decorate with crystalised cherries and strips of angelica; fill three-quarters full with the rice mixture. Bake for three-quarters of an hour and turn, and serve the sauce (Recipe No. 17) with them.

Strawberries and Cream in Winter.

INGREDIENTS:

Bananas.
Strawberry jam.

Whipped cream.
Huntley and Palmer's wafers.

Cut some nice fresh bananas in thin slices and put at the bottom of little glasses or tiny old china basins. Next put a layer of strawberry jam, and lastly fill up with whipped cream. Serve in silver dish, with a spoon to each, and hand wafers with them.

Jubilee Pudding.

INGREDIENTS:

1½ lbs. breadcrumbs.
1¼ pints new milk.
4 eggs.

3 ozs. butter.
1 lemon.
3 ozs. caster sugar.

Mix the breadcrumbs with the milk, butter, and

sugar, then add the yolks of four eggs, well beaten, and the juice of a lemon. Put all into a buttered pie-dish, and bake until a nice brown, then take out and spread a thick layer of apricot jam on the top, and lastly the whites of the eggs, that have been beaten to a stiff froth. Put the pudding back into the oven until the whites are set and a golden brown. This is very nice cold or hot.

Tapioca Cream.

INGREDIENTS:

1 pint milk.
Teacupful of tapioca.
2 eggs.

Jam.
Vanilla.
Teacupful of caster sugar.

Place over the fire an enamel stewpan, with one pint of milk and a teacupful of tapioca and sugar. Boil until quite soft. Meanwhile beat the eggs well. When the tapioca is well done, put it into a basin, and when nearly cold add the eggs and a little vanilla flavouring, and beat all together until it comes to a cream. Put it into a glass dish (which has a layer of jam at the bottom) with whipped cream on the top and chopped pistachio nuts over.

Apricots and Rice à la Snow.

INGREDIENTS:

Rice.
Vanilla.
Apricots.

Sugar:
Cream.

Prepare the rice as you would for rice mould; put

it into a round, white, china souffle mould. When set turn out carefully in centre of round silver dish. Place on the top of the rice half apricots, overlapping each other, with a preserved cherry on the top of each one. Pour some of the syrup of the apricots round, and fill up the centre of apricots with whipped cream. This can be served either hot or cold.

Zéphyrs de Semolina.

INGREDIENTS :

Teacupful of semolina. | Caster sugar.
3 eggs.

For a pint mould take about half a teacupful of semolina and leave it to soak in water. Then drain off, and mix it with three whites of eggs, well beaten to a stiff froth, and the yolk of one egg, also well beaten, a little caster sugar, and any flavouring, if liked. Beat all well together and pour into a buttered mould, and steam for two or three hours. Turn out, and serve with French custard.

Lop-lollie.

INGREDIENTS :

Ground rice. | Jam.
1 pint of milk.

Boil half a teacupful of ground rice in about one pint of milk until quite cooked and stiff. Serve in glass dish, with jam or fruit.

Christmas Plum-pudding. (*The best.*)

INGREDIENTS:

3 lbs. of breadcrumbs.
1 lb. of flour.
3 lbs. of finely shred suet.
3 lbs. of raisins (stoned).
3 lbs. of sultanas.
3 lbs. of currants.
3 lbs. of Demerara sugar.
3 nutmegs (grated),

2 lbs. of mixed chopped peel.
The juice of 2 lemons and rind of 3.
2 lbs. of sweet almonds (blanched and chopped).
1 oz. of salt.
32 eggs.
½ bottle of best brandy.

First well mix all the dry ingredients in a large pan. Then add the eggs, the yolks to be beaten separately from the whites, and the whites to a stiff froth. Then add the brandy, and if the mixture is too stiff add a little beer. This will make a very large pudding, and wants boiling for twelve hours, but it will also make thirteen good-sized puddings. Have the basins well buttered and sugared, then fill up with the mixture, not quite to the top. Then have rounds of buttered and sugared papers to fit the basins, and cover each with ; lastly, tie each basin up tightly in a floured cloth, bringing the four corners up on the top, which tie in a knot. Boil for at least twelve hours. These puddings will keep twelve months. When wanted boil for five or six hours. Serve with brandy cream sauce.

Marigolds.

INGREDIENTS:

Puff paste.
Apricot jam.

Caster sugar.
White of egg.

Make some best puff paste and roll out about a

quarter of an inch thick into a large square piece. Cut into small squares, about two inches in size, and just wet the centre of the squares with a drop of water, and fold the four corners over into the centre. Brush over with the white of an egg, and sprinkle white sugar over. Bake in a nice hot oven for fifteen minutes. If to be served hot, place a spoonful of hot apricot jam on the top, and a spoonful of whipped cream. If to be cold, put cold jam, and then the cream. The marigolds ought only to be large enough for one mouthful.

Chocolate Pudding.

INGREDIENTS:

3 ozs. of flour, chocolate, and sugar.
2 ozs. of butter.

½ pint of cream or milk.
4 eggs.

Let the butter melt in an enamel stewpan, then add the cream and flour. Stir well, and cook for ten minutes. Then add the sugar and grated chocolate and the yolks of three eggs, well beaten, and then the whites of four eggs, beaten to a stiff froth. Stir all well lightly, and pour into a prepared souffle mould; steam for one hour, and serve very hot. Hand some cream in a silver jug.

Swiss Roll.

INGREDIENTS:

4 eggs.
1 breakfastcupful of flour.
1 breakfastcupful caster sugar.
Vanilla essence to taste.

1 teaspoonful of cream of tartar.
1 teaspoonful of carbonate of soda.

Dissolve the carbonate of soda in a tablespoonful

of milk or water. Put into a basin the flour, sugar, cream of tartar, and vanilla essence, and beat all together lightly with the eggs, which have been previously well beaten; lastly add the carbonate of soda. Pour the batter on to a well-buttered baking-sheet, and bake in a quick oven for ten minutes. Turn out on to a sugared paper, spread with hot jam, and roll up.

You can either make a large roll, or twelve little rolls, about three inches long and one and a half inches round. These little rolls look very nice iced with pink and white icing.

Custard in Jelly.

INGREDIENTS:

Jelly. | Custard.
Gelatine. |

Take about half a pint of clear jelly and melt it. Make a pint of custard, then add $\frac{1}{2}$ oz. of gelatine, which has been previously soaked. Stir until dissolved. Then divide the custard into three parts, and leave one yellow, colour one pink and another chocolate. Put into three soup-plates to set; when set cut up in small square pieces. Put a little jelly in the bottom of the tin, fill up with the custard. Pour in the jelly, and let it set. When cold turn out.

Lemon Cheesecakes.

INGREDIENTS:

$\frac{1}{2}$ lb. of butter. | Rind of two lemons, grated,
$\frac{1}{2}$ lb. of caster sugar. | and a little juice.
2 eggs, and a few currants. |

Beat the butter and sugar well together, then add

the eggs, well beaten, lastly add the lemon-rind and currants.

Urney Pudding.

INGREDIENTS:

Weight of two eggs in flour.
Weight of one egg in castor sugar.
Weight of two eggs in butter.
1 saltspoonful of carbonate of soda.

Beat the butter to a cream, mix in the sugar, add one egg, and beat well together. Then add the other egg. Mix the soda well with the flour, and shake in while stirring. Then add about three tablespoonfuls of strawberry jam. Put in a buttered mould and steam for two and a half hours.

A quickly made Sweet.

INGREDIENTS:

Sponge cake.
Custard.
Cream.

Fill some little glass custard cups (with or without handles) three parts full of sponge cake. Make a nice custard, flavoured well, and while hot pour over the sponge cake and fill up the cups. When cold drop a lump of whipped cream on each, and sprinkle with finely chopped pistachio nuts. Serve in a silver dish, with a spoon for each.

VII
SAVOURIES—HOT AND COLD

Fried Sardines.

INGREDIENTS :

Sardines.
Egg.
Breadcrumbs.

Lard.
Lemon.

EMPTY a tin of sardines, and remove most carefully their skin and bone. Next egg-and-breadcrumb them exactly as you would smelts. Fry them in boiling lard in a frying basket until a light brown. Dish up in a hot silver dish, and serve brown bread-and-butter and cut lemon with them.

Tomato Savoury.

INGREDIENTS :

Tomatoes.
Chives.
Chili vinegar.

Pepper.
Egg.

Peel some English tomatoes, and chop them up finely with the chopped chives, pepper, chili vinegar, and mix with this a well-beaten egg. Fry all together in boiling butter, and serve on fried *croûtons* of bread, very hot, with a hot *purée* of tomatoes in centre of the dish.

Eggs and Anchovies.

INGREDIENTS :

2 eggs.
4 anchovies (boned in oil).

Bread-and-butter.
Cucumber.

Have some long strips of bread-and-butter, then put through a fine sieve the hard-boiled eggs until the bread is thickly covered, and drop some Harvey sauce on it carefully. Then lay some boned anchovies, cut in slices, slant-ways across the egg, then some cucumber, also cut in slices, across the anchovies in the opposite direction.

Cheese Sticks.

INGREDIENTS :

Cheese.
Butter.
Chili vinegar.

Cayenne pepper.
Batter.

Take little lengths of good rich cheese about the size of your little finger, soaked for an hour or so in oiled butter liberally flavoured with chili vinegar and cayenne pepper. Then dip each finger into batter and fry in the basket for a few minutes. Pile high in hot silver dish on fancy dish paper, and serve as cheese course, with celery or watercress handed with them.

Shrimps and Green Butter.

INGREDIENTS :

Picked brown or pink shrimps.
Green butter.

Boned anchovies.
Bread-and-butter.

Cut some rounds of bread-and-butter ; make a

pyramid of green butter on each. Stick the picked shrimps on the bread-and-butter all round. Put strips of anchovies going up the green butter, ending at top with a sprig of chervil.

Mushrooms and Marrow on Toast.

INGREDIENTS :

Mushrooms.
Marrow from marrow bone.
Lemon-juice.

Pepper and salt.
Finely chopped parsley.

Cook the mushrooms carefully until quite tender (mushrooms all the same size, if possible, about as large as a five-shilling piece), then put one on a piece of hot fried bread the size of the mushroom, and fill up the centre of each with hot marrow flavoured with lemon-juice, pepper and salt, and a little chopped parsley. Serve in silver dish, very hot.

Cod's Roe.

INGREDIENTS :

Cold boiled cod's roe.
Bread-and-butter.

Pepper and salt.

Cut some thin strips of new bread-and-butter, and cut the cod's roe very thin and fry in butter for a few minutes until quite hot. Arrange the roe on the bread-and-butter, and pepper each. Dish up nicely and garnish with parsley.

Shrimps à la Mayonnaise.

INGREDIENTS:

1 pint of picked shrimps.	Mayonnaise sauce.
Bread-and-butter.	Chopped chives or parsley.

Take the shrimps and put into a thick mayonnaise sauce, then spread on bread-and-butter or buttered toast (cut in any shape or form), and sprinkle with chives or parsley chopped very fine.

Prawns and Mayonnaise. (*Very Pretty.*)

INGREDIENTS:

Mayonnaise sauce.	Bread-and-butter.
12 prawns.	Cucumber.
Coral.	

Cut six slices of bread-and-butter, or buttered toast if preferred, diamond shape. Spread thickly with stiff mayonnaise sauce, and place a peeled prawn up at each corner of the diamond. Between each prawn put a thin slice of cucumber sticking out, and in the centre the head of the prawn and some parsley.

Prawns and Anchovy Butter.

INGREDIENTS:

8 Prawns (peeled).	Cucumber.
Anchovy butter.	Bread-and-butter.

Cut rounds of bread-and-butter, spread the butter very thick, lay the prawns on in turn, filling up the tail of each with anchovy butter, standing nice and high. Place in the centre of all the prawn's head, and garnish the dish with slices of cucumber soaked in chili vinegar.

Sardines à la Surprise.

INGREDIENTS :

Egg.
Sardines.
Half a glass of sherry.

Half a glass of salad oil.
1 oz. flour.

Make a batter out of the sherry, salad oil, and flour. Make it thick enough to dip the sardines into, then dip each sardine in the white of an egg, and fry very crisp and light. Dish up on lengths of hot fried bread, and serve in a silver dish.

Devilled Shrimps.

INGREDIENTS :

Shrimps (picked).
Butter.

Cayenne pepper.
Parsley.

Roll the shrimps in a floured cloth until well covered, then fry them in boiling butter for a minute. Then turn them on to a sieve and dust with cayenne pepper. Serve very hot on rounds of fried bread, and garnish with parsley.

Chicken Liver Savoury.

INGREDIENTS :

Butter.
Gravy.
Bread (fried).

Bacon.
Lemon-juice.

Melt the butter in a saucepan and add a tablespoonful of gravy to each liver (one chicken liver makes enough for four people). Cook for ten minutes, then chop it up finely. Have ready some rounds of hot fried bread, on which place a piece of hot fried bacon. Pile the chopped liver up high on each piece of bacon, and put into the oven to get very hot. Dish up down centre of a silver dish, and just before serving squeeze a little lemon-juice on each. Garnish with tomato *purée* on each.

Aigrettes of Parmesan.

INGREDIENTS:

¼ pint water.	2 ozs. of grated cheese.
2 ozs. of butter.	2 eggs.
2 ozs. of flour.	Pepper and salt.

Put the butter into a saucepan with the water. Let it boil, shake in the flour and cook well. Add the cheese and the eggs, well beaten, one at a time. Have ready some boiling fat and drop in about a dessertspoonful of the mixture at a time. Fry a golden brown, and serve, piled up, very hot, in a silver dish, and sprinkle finely grated cheese over them and a little pepper.

Yellow and Green Butter-baskets.

INGREDIENTS:

2 eggs.	Marshall's liquid sap-green colouring.
Anchovy sauce.	
Chili vinegar.	

Boil the eggs hard, and when done put into cold water for a few minutes. Peel carefully and cut the end off each egg. Cut them in half and take out the yolks. Put the yolks of the eggs in separate mortars. Pound up one yolk with anchovy sauce, pepper, chili vinegar and a little butter, and a few drops of Marshall's sap-green. Pound the other yolk up with chopped onion, a little butter, and flavour with Harvey's sauce. Fill up two whites of eggs with the yellow butter and two with green butter. Put on rounds of bread and butter, garnish with handles of chives.

Anchovy Cream Savoury.

INGREDIENTS:

1 gill of cream.
Cheese biscuits, or cream cracknels.

Anchovy sauce.
Boned anchovies in oil.

Have some cold cheese biscuits or some cracknel biscuits spread with whipped cream (which has been mixed with anchovy sauce), and curl a boned anchovy on each, with an olive in the centre. Decorate nicely.

Cheese Biscuits, or Cheese Straws.

INGREDIENTS:

3 ozs. butter.
3 ozs. flour.
4 ozs. grated cheese.

Pepper and salt.
1 egg.

Mix the butter, flour, cheese (either Cheddar or Parmesan will do), salt and pepper into a dough, with the yolk of the egg, and a little water if too stiff. Roll out thin on a floured board, and cut into thin strips, for straws, and cut a few rings. Bake in a hot oven for about ten minutes. The straws should be made into little bundles and placed through the rings. If for cheese biscuits, simply cut with a round cutter any size you may like.

Moelle de bœuf aux Tomates.

INGREDIENTS :

Beef marrow. | Tomato sauce.
Batter. |

Cut some beef marrow into two-inch lengths. Dip in batter and fry for two or three minutes. Serve very hot with tomato sauce.

Olives à la Métropole.

INGREDIENTS :

Olives. | Aspic.
Green butter. | Bologna sausages.

Take as many olives as guests. Stone them and stuff with green butter. Set each in a little mould with aspic jelly. When cold, turn out and serve each on a slice of Bologna sausage. Garnish with green butter at the edge.

Croûtes à la Clarisse.

INGREDIENTS :

Toast. | Bacon.
Ham. | Batter.
Anchovy. |

Take some thin slices of fat bacon, and roll up in

each some pounded ham and anchovy. Dip in batter and fry a few minutes. Serve piled up high in a hot silver dish, garnished with parsley.

Cheese Marbles.

INGREDIENTS:

2 eggs (whites only).	Salt.
Cheese.	Cayenne pepper.

Beat up the whites of the eggs to a stiff froth. Stir in about two tablespoonfuls of grated cheese, a little salt, and cayenne pepper. Shape into balls about the size of marbles, and drop each into boiling fat. Fry until a golden colour, and serve all piled up, in the hollow of an oval piece of bread cut thick and previously fried. Garnish with parsley.

Macaroni and Tomatoes.

INGREDIENTS:

Macaroni.	Cayenne pepper.
Salt.	Butter.
Sherry.	½ lb. grated cheese.

Boil the macaroni until quite tender in salt and water, and let it drain. Make it tasty with a little sherry and cayenne pepper and a few little pieces of butter. Then put it into the basin in which it is to be served. Make a good tomato sauce, add a little cream, and the grated cheese (any kind). Mix well, and boil, stirring all the time, then take a little of it and mix into the macaroni, stirring it round and round, then just before sending it to table pour the rest of the sauce smoothly over the top, and serve at once. Delicious.

Œufs à la Brentmore.

INGREDIENTS:

2 tomatoes.	Hard-boiled eggs.
Tarragon vinegar.	Chopped chives.

Cut little buttered rounds of freshly made toast. Peel and slice the tomatoes about half an inch thick, and drop tarragon vinegar on them. Place first a slice of tomato on the toast, then a thin slice of hard-boiled egg. Sprinkle chopped chives over the egg. Serve in silver dish, with parsley on a dish-paper.

Devilled Sardine Butter.

INGREDIENTS:

6 sardines.	Chili vinegar.
Bread-and-butter.	Red pepper.

Cut six little rounds of bread-and-butter, about the size of a five-shilling piece. Pound five boned sardines in a mortar, with a lump of fresh butter, flavour with chili vinegar and red pepper. Spread the sardine butter on the rounds of bread-and-butter, and cut in strips the other sardine, boned. Decorate with chervil or parsley.

Macaroni Cheese.

INGREDIENTS:

Macaroni.
Pepper.

Béchamel sauce.
Grated cheese.

First soak and boil in water until tender enough macaroni as will be required to nearly fill your dish. Then put it in the white Béchamel sauce, well flavoured with grated cheese, pepper, and a little mustard. Fill your fireproof fancy dish, and sprinkle cheese thickly over the top, and put a little lump of butter here and there. Bake in a hot oven for twenty minutes or half an hour. Serve very hot.

Ham and Egg Toast.

INGREDIENTS:

3 ozs. ham (remains).
Eggs, hard-boiled.
Butter.

Pepper and salt.
Toast.

Pound the ham quite smoothly in a mortar, also the butter and the yolk of the egg. Add pepper and salt, and any flavouring that is liked. Spread on rounds of hot buttered toast, and garnish with the white of the egg chopped very fine.

Egg and Tomato Savoury.

INGREDIENTS:

1½ ozs. butter.
1 onion.

Tomatoes.
3 eggs.

Put into a saucepan the butter and onion chopped

very fine. Cook the onion until tender, and add a little cold ham or tongue that has been chopped fine. Let all get hot, then add the slices of tomatoes that have been peeled. Then stir in three raw eggs, and stir until the eggs begin to set. Then dish up on squares of buttered toast, and serve very hot.

Sardines à la Toby.

INGREDIENTS :

| Sardines. | Chili vinegar. |
| Slices of bacon. | Hard-boiled egg. |

Scrape and bone the sardines carefully. Take out the bone, and put in a few drops of chili vinegar, and chopped-up hard-boiled egg. Form the fish again, and wrap each one up in a piece of fat bacon. Lay each one on a piece of hot buttered toast, the length and shape of the sardine, and put on a tin in a hot oven, and leave until the bacon is done. Take out and dish up on a hot silver dish, and serve at once.

Scrambled Sardines.

INGREDIENTS :

Sardines (boned).	1 or 2 eggs.
Chili vinegar.	Butter.
Coraline pepper.	Chopped capers.

Break the sardines up with a fork, flavouring with chili vinegar and coraline pepper. Have the egg well beaten up in a basin with a whisk, and mix with the sardines. Put some fresh butter to boil in an omelette pan, and when boiling stir in the eggs and sardines. When done serve on rounds of hot buttered toast, and garnish with chopped capers and parsley.

Anchovy Parcels.

INGREDIENTS :

Cheese straw mixture. | Anchovies (boned).

Make some cheese straw mixture, and roll out rather thin. Cut the paste into oblong pieces about three inches by two inches. Lay on the paste a boned, oiled anchovy, then roll up the paste, entirely enveloping the anchovy. Bake in a hot oven until a golden colour, and pile the anchovy parcels up high, crossways, in a silver dish. Serve either hot or cold, but it is best hot.

Cauliflower au Gratin.

INGREDIENTS :

Cauliflower.
Grated cheese (Parmesan and Gruyère).
Melted butter.
Breadcrumbs.
Pepper.

Well clean a nice cauliflower in salt and water, dry it thoroughly, and put it into a fireproof dish well buttered. Have ready a beautiful white sauce, with plenty of pepper and grated cheese mixed in it. Pour the sauce over the cauliflower, and sprinkle finely grated breadcrumbs over it, and put little lumps of butter over it. Bake in a hot oven until the whole is coloured a light brown. Serve on a folded napkin, and decorate with parsley.

Ramequins.

INGREDIENTS:

¼ lb. good cheese (grated).
3 eggs.
Milk or cream.
Salt.

Cayenne pepper.
Puff pastry, or little paper cases.
Butter.

Grate the cheese, beat up three eggs, and stir in with the milk or cream. Add salt and cayenne. The mixture must be of the consistency of cream. Line some patty-pans with puff paste, and just as you are putting them into the oven fill them with this mixture, and place a small piece of butter on each. The oven must be very hot, as these ramequins must only bake for ten minutes. Serve immediately. If paper cases are used they must be well buttered before the mixture is put into them; they will take the same time to cook.

To use up Eggs.

If you want the yolks only of an egg for decorating chicken, salads, savouries, &c., break one carefully, and separate the white from the yolk, then put the yolk carefully into boiling water and boil for five minutes, then it is ready for use. The fresh white will help to make meringues, or for doing over cutlets, or for egg and breadcrumbs. Then if the white is required and not the yolk, boil the white in the same manner and use the yolk for anything you may want it for.

VIII

SAUCES, ICING, &c.

(WRINKLE)

A tin of Nelson's extract of meat, dissolved in two tablespoonfuls of boiling water, will make a good glaze for tongues, or for adding to sauces where told.

Chocolate Icing.

To ¾ lb. of icing sugar add ½ lb. of fresh butter, a ¼ lb. of finely powdered chocolate, and about half a wineglass of brandy or liqueur. Mix all well together with a wooden spoon for about fifteen minutes, when it will present a creamy appearance, and is ready for use.

Chocolate Glaze.

Put into a stewpan 2 ozs. of finely-grated Fry's vanilla chocolate, with a quarter pint of water, and cook till smooth. Then mix with it 1 lb. of icing sugar and three tablespoonfuls of warm water. Just warm it up and pour over the cakes.

Plain Syrup for Stewing whole Pears or Apples in.

Half a pound loaf sugar, three-quarters pint of water. Boil until reduced to half. Then add the fruit pared and cored, whole or in halves.

Icing for Genoese Pastry.

Half a pound of icing sugar, juice of one lemon

and a little cold water. Pass the sugar through a hair sieve, put it into a saucepan with the lemon-juice and water. Let it get hot, but not boil, and use it.

Batter for Frying (*sufficient to make a quarter of a pint*).

Mix 5 ozs. of flour, with one gill of warm water, into a paste. Add two tablespoonfuls of salad oil, and just before using stir in the whites of two eggs beaten to a stiff froth.

To Clarify Dripping.

Take the dripping while hot, after having fried anything, and pour it into a basin half full of hot water, and stir well, and leave until the morning.

Savoury Custard.

Ingredients:

1 egg.	Pepper and salt.
Chopped parsley.	

Beat the white and yolk of the egg separately, and then together. Stir in a little chopped parsley, pepper and salt to taste. Butter some small moulds, pour in the custard, and bake for ten minutes. Turn out and cut into pretty shapes, and put into good clear soup where directed.

Wine Sauce for Puddings.

INGREDIENTS:

1 tablespoonful of any jam.	1 gill of cold water.
1 oz. of loaf sugar.	Juice of a lemon.

Boil altogether for a few minutes, and just before serving stir in a glass of sherry or a tablespoonful of whisky or brandy.

Horseradish Sauce.

Scrape very finely indeed as much horseradish as required, and add it to half a pint of whipped cream and also a little salt and a few drops of chili vinegar.

Sauce for Ragout of Cold Game, Meat, Chicken, or Duck.

INGREDIENTS:

Shallot.	½ a pint of stock.
Flour.	Red-currant jelly.
Butter.	

Chop up the shallot and put an ounce of butter, with the same of flour, and fry until a nice brown. Then add a small pot of red-currant jelly, or a glass of port wine, a tablespoonful of Worcester sauce, half a pint of any stock you may have, and stir until thick but smooth. Then it is ready for any cold meat to be put into it until quite hot. Serve in a silver dish, with fried potatoes in the middle.

Dutch Sauce for Meat and Fish.

INGREDIENTS:

2 or 3 eggs.
Vinegar.

½ a lemon.

Put six tablespoonfuls of water and four of vinegar into a saucepan. Make it hot and thicken with the yolks of two or three eggs. Make it quite hot, but not to boil. Squeeze the juice from half a lemon, strain it through a sieve, and serve in a tureen.

Tomato Sauce for Keeping.

INGREDIENTS:

4 lbs. ripe tomatoes
2 onions.
Salt.

Peppercorns.
Allspice.

Cut the tomatoes into slices and put them into a stewpan, with two large onions sliced, 1 lb. of Demerara sugar, ¼ lb. of salt, 2 ozs. peppercorns, half a teaspoonful of cayenne pepper, ½ oz. of allspice, and the same of cloves. Pour a pint of vinegar over the ingredients, and let them boil gently for two hours. Stir frequently to prevent them from burning. Rub them through a fine sieve, and as soon as the pulp is cold bottle it securely and store in a cool, dry place.

Brandy Cream Sauce.

INGREDIENTS:

1 pint cream
Brandy.

3 ozs. of sweet almonds.

Whip up the cream and add a wineglass of

brandy, and 3 ozs. of finely chopped sweet almonds. Of course any quantity can be used more or less for this particular recipe.

Sauce for Haddock.

INGREDIENTS :

4 tablespoonfuls of French vinegar.
1 sprig of thyme.
3 bay-leaves
12 crushed peppercorns.

4 yolks of eggs.
¼ lb. fresh butter.
6 tablespoonfuls of tomato sauce (recipe given).

Put the vinegar, thyme, bay-leaves, and crushed peppercorns into a stewpan. Reduce it to half the quantity, then add the yolks of the eggs, and by degrees the fresh butter, standing the pot in the bain-marie, or in a pan of boiling water. Stir until it thickens, add six tablespoonfuls of boiling tomato sauce.

Tomato Sauce.

INGREDIENTS :

4 tomatoes.
1 onion.
1 carrot.
¼ lb. butter.

2 tablespoonfuls of vinegar.
¼ pint of stock.
2 lumps of sugar.

Cut the tomatoes, onion, and carrots into pieces. Put them in a stewpan with the butter, vinegar, and stock. Stew until the vegetables are tender. Then rub all through a wire sieve and then through a hair sieve, and add it, or part of it, to the fish sauce (recipe given), and the remainder will do to flavour any fish sauce or soup or gravy next day.

Sauce Hollandaise.

INGREDIENTS :

½ pint of white sauce.
3 eggs.
¼ lb. oiled butter.
2 lemons (juice only).

Pepper and salt.
2 teaspoonfuls of chili vinegar.
1 gill of thick cream.

Make half a pint of best white sauce, and when boiling stir in off the fire the yolk of the eggs, then add the butter oiled (not too hot), keep it well stirred over the fire until it thickens; do not let it boil. Then add the juice of two lemons, pepper, salt, and chili vinegar, and just before sending in stir in the cream.

Sauce for Rice Moulds.

INGREDIENTS :

1 oz. butter.
1 dessertspoonful of flour.
½ pint milk.

1 oz. sugar.
Wineglass of sherry.

Melt the butter and rub in the flour with a wooden spoon, add the sugar and milk, and let it boil until it thickens. Add the sherry, and pour over the moulds.

Caramel.

INGREDIENTS :

Loaf sugar

Broth or water.

Take some pounded loaf sugar, browned in a saucepan over the fire, moistened with a little water or broth, and stirred with a fork all the while.

Great care must be taken not to burn it. When sufficiently browned it may be stored away in a jar. Its use is to smear with a feather or brush over the surface of cooked meats, to glaze or colour them, and also to make sauces and gravies look richer by deepening their colour.

Windsor Sauce.

INGREDIENTS:

Wineglass of tarragon vinegar. | 2 ozs. of butter.
2 yolks of eggs. | 2 tablespoonfuls of white sauce.

Reduce the tarragon vinegar to half the quantity. Add the yolks of the eggs, the butter, and the white sauce, sprinkle a little chopped in it before serving.

Tar-Tar Sauce.

INGREDIENTS:

Melted butter. | Tarragon.
Stock. | Capers.
Chutney.

Make some melted butter, but instead of using milk or water use a little nicely flavoured brown stock, adding a little chutney, a little chopped tarragon, and some whole capers. Mix well, and serve very hot.

"Donna Lol" Sauce to eat with Green Artichokes.

INGREDIENTS:

Eggs. | Tarragon vinegar.
Melted butter.

Make some melted butter with milk or cream.

Beat up the yolk of one egg, and into it add some black pepper, a little salt, and about six or eight drops of tarragon vinegar. Serve very hot in a tureen.

Toosie Sauce.

Mince two onions or shallots very fine, and fry in butter with a little flour and half a pint of stock. Add to this some finely chopped capers, parsley, tarragon, and mushrooms. Mix in a little mustard, pepper, salt, and sugar to taste, and a little allspice. Let all boil well, and just before serving add a small lump of butter. Mind all is a good dark colour; a little chili vinegar can be added if liked.

Piquant Sauce.

Put a pint of vinegar (or half if only a little sauce is required), with a chopped-up onion, and garlic or shallot, a bunch of sweet herbs, chopped fine, and pepper and salt to taste; add a little allspice. Let all these ingredients boil gently for about three-quarters of an hour. Then melt about 1 oz. of butter, and stir in a little flour, then pour in the vinegar, which must be carefully strained, and add about half a pint of stock. Let all come to the boil, stirring all the time, then it is ready for use.

Ordinary Thick Brown Sauce.

Chop up an onion or two finely, and fry in a little butter until a good dark brown, then add a little flour. Stir all into the stock you are going to make your sauce of, and flavour with Worcester or Harvey sauce, or a little mushroom ketchup.

White Sauce.

Melt a lump of butter with a little flour, mix smoothly, then add some milk or white stock. Let it boil until it is the right thickness, then stir in the yolks of two or three eggs and a little lemon-juice. Pepper and salt to taste.

Shrimp Sauce.

Make a nice melted butter, and add the flesh of some freshly picked shrimps, that have been pounded in a mortar with a little mace, a lump of butter, and a few drops of anchovy sauce. Stir all until smooth and very hot, and serve.

Bread Sauce.

Boil in half a pint of milk an onion stuck with cloves, a blade of mace, and a few peppercorns, until the milk is nicely flavoured. Add a little pepper and salt to taste. Strain the milk and pour it on to 2 ozs. of breadcrumbs. Make all hot, stir in a lump of fresh butter, and serve.

Egg Sauce.

Make good, well-flavoured melted butter, and add a little cream. Have two or three hard-boiled eggs, chopped very fine, and stir into the melted butter.

Mayonnaise Sauce.

INGREDIENTS:

Egg.
Mustard.
Salad oil.
Chili vinegar.

Break into a basin the yolk of an egg, add a pinch of salt, raw mustard, and pepper. With a wooden spoon stir in the salad oil, which must be dropped in slowly, as the sauce should be quite thick and smooth when you have added about three tablespoonfuls of oil. Add slowly a little chili vinegar, and on the top some finely chopped chives. If you want much sauce use two or three eggs. The whites whipped to a very stiff froth, and a little pepper and vinegar added looks very pretty piled high on the yellow mayonnaise sauce, and the green chopped chives sprinkled over them.

Sauce for Fish.

INGREDIENTS:

2 eggs. | Melted butter.

Make a pint of melted butter, add the yolks of two eggs, well beaten, and stir quickly over the fire until it thickens, but do not let it boil. Flavour well with pepper and salt, and it is ready for use.

IX

HORS D'ŒUVRES

German Sausage.

INGREDIENTS :

Bologna sausage.
Mustard butter.
Mustard and cress.

Egg.
Bread-and-butter.

CUT some thin slices of sausage and form a sandwich with two slices, spreading thickly with mustard butter and chopped mustard and cress. Lay each sandwich on a round of bread-and-butter, and place on the top the yolk of a hard-boiled egg, rubbed through a sieve.

Anchovy Tastes.

INGREDIENTS :

Anchovy butter.
Olives.

Bread-and-butter.

Stone some olives and fill each with anchovy butter, and place each olive on a slice of hard-boiled guinea fowl's egg, and place a picked pink shrimp coming out of the top of the olive.

Lobster Pots.

INGREDIENTS :

Lobster. Cucumber butter.
Anchovy sauce. Cayenne pepper.

Take all the meat out of a nice lobster and cut up into small pieces and sprinkle with cayenne pepper. Half fill some tiny white soufflé moulds with very rich anchovy sauce; fill up with the lobster and decorate the top of each with cucumber *purée*. Serve one to each guest, and serve a tiny roll of brown bread-and-butter with each.

Sardine Creams.

INGREDIENTS :

Sardines. Bread-and-butter.
Whipped cream.

Cut some rounds of bread-and-butter, and cover each with mashed and boned sardines that have been flavoured with chili vinegar or lemon-juice and pepper. Drop on top of that a lump of whipped cream, and sprinkle the coral from a lobster over all. Bake the lobster coral first and rub through a very fine sieve.

Tomato Cups.

INGREDIENTS :

Mayonnaise sauce. Bread-and-butter.
Pepper. Whipped cream.
Cucumber.

Take little round English tomatoes, one for each

guest. Take off the top of each and scrape out all the middle, mix the tomato with some mayonnaise sauce, cayenne pepper, and Worcester sauce. Fill up each tomato skin again, and serve with a lump of whipped cream on the top. Place each tomato cup on a round of bread-and-butter and a thin slice of cucumber.

Sardines à la Royal.

INGREDIENTS:

Sardines.
Mustard and cress, or chervil.
Chili vinegar.

Cucumber.
Beetroot.
Bread-and-butter.

Skin and bone the sardines without spoiling their shape, drop some chili vinegar on the fish when you remove the bone and close up again. Place each sardine on a piece of bread-and-butter cut the same shape as the sardine, and decorate with strips of the white of a hard-boiled egg and strips of cucumber and beetroot alternately. Serve one to each guest, on a tiny white plate, with a little chervil or mustard and cress round.

Anchovies.

INGREDIENTS:

Anchovies.
Bread-and-butter.

Olives.

Cut as many small rounds of bread-and-butter as there are guests. Place a stoned olive in centre of each round, and wind a boned anchovy round each olive, and place at the top a tiny sprig of chervil.

Oysters.

INGREDIENTS :

Oysters.
Vinegar.

Pepper.

Place the oysters in the deep shell of the oyster, and drop a few drops of chili vinegar and cayenne pepper on each. Serve a half-dozen to each guest, with thin slices of bread-and-butter.

Caviare.

INGREDIENTS :

Caviare.
Toast.

Butter.

Cut some rounds of toast three different sizes, beginning about one and a half inches across. Spread fresh butter on each and caviare, and then put the three pieces together to form a small pyramid. Serve one to each guest.

Bloater Roes.

INGREDIENTS :

Bloater roes.
Butter.
Anchovy sauce.

Pepper.
Hard-boiled egg.

Take some soft or hard bloater roes and pound in the mortar with lemon-juice, cayenne pepper, a few drops of anchovy sauce, and a small lump of butter. Have some small diamond-shaped pieces of fried bread, cold, and spread the mixture on each. Decorate with the white of a hard-boiled egg put through a fine sieve.

Devilled Prawns.

INGREDIENTS :

| Prawns. | Mayonnaise sauce. |
| Cayenne pepper. | Bread-and-butter. |

Cut some heart-shaped pieces of bread-and-butter, and stick up all round some fresh prawns, which marinade in anchovy sauce and chili vinegar for an hour or so. Fill up the centre of prawns with thick devilled mayonnaise sauce and a sprig of fried parsley on top of each, and sprinkle well with red pepper.

X
BREAD, FANCY BREADS, CAKES AND BISCUITS

(WRINKLE)

Macdougall's self-raising flour is the best for all kinds of cakes and pastry, and requires no baking powder.

Bread.

INGREDIENTS :

| Flour. | Caster sugar. |
| German yeast. | Salt. |

PUT 3 lbs. of flour into a basin, with two teaspoonfuls of salt and a dessertspoonful of caster sugar, if liked. Mix it all well together, and dissolve 1 oz. of fresh German yeast in a teacupful of cold water. Make a hole in the middle of the flour and pour this in. Then add as much hot water (the heat of which should be about what you could bear your finger in) as will make the dough a very nice elastic consistency. Knead for five or six minutes. Then make it into loaves, and put into well-greased tins to rise for an hour, or until the dough has risen well. It is best to stand the tins on the hot-plate rack over the stove, and cover them over with a cloth. When ready, put them into a nice hot oven to begin with, and then gradually slacken off. When done, turn the loaves out of the tins, and let them lie bottom upwards until they are cold.

Duncroft Cakes.

INGREDIENTS:

1 lb. flour.
½ lb. of butter
2 eggs.

6 ozs. of white sugar.
3 ozs. of almonds, chopped.
Vanilla.

Whip the butter to a cream with your hand, then add the sugar, the flour, and the almonds. Mix in the eggs, well beaten to a stiff paste in a basin, and then shape the mixture into little cakes with a teaspoon. Arrange them on a baking-tin, sugar them, and bake in a quick oven. These are quite delicious; and the vanilla must be added to the eggs when beaten, about a teaspoonful of essence of vanilla to 1 lb. of flour.

Little Queen Cakes, for tea.

INGREDIENTS:

¼ lb. of butter.
¼ lb. of sugar.
2 eggs.

¼ lb. of flour.
1 oz. of currants or sultanas.

Beat the butter to a cream, and add the sugar, a little nutmeg, and vanilla essence. Beat in the two eggs, which should have been well beaten together, and then add the currants and flour. Mix all well together, and drop a little into small buttered patty or cake tins. Bake in a hot oven for a quarter of an hour. This quantity will make about thirty-six cakes.

Madeira Cake.

INGREDIENTS :

4½ ozs. of flour.
3 ozs. of sugar.
3 ozs. of butter.
3 eggs.

1 teaspoonful baking powder.
Flavour with essence of lemon
  to taste.

Beat the sugar and butter to a cream, then add the flour by degrees, and yolks of eggs well beaten, then add the whites, beaten to a stiff froth. Lastly add the baking powder and essence of lemon. Beat all well together for five minutes. Bake for one hour.

Gingerbread Cake.

INGREDIENTS :

1½ lbs. of flour.
1 lb. of treacle.
¼ lb. of butter.
¼ lb. of sugar.
¼ pint of warm milk.

1 oz. of ginger.
1 teaspoonful of carbonate of
  soda.
3 eggs.

Mix the flour, sugar, and ginger together. Warm the treacle, dissolve the soda in the milk, and mix all well together. Add the eggs last, and bake from three-quarters to one hour.

Sponge Cake.

INGREDIENTS :

7 eggs.
Boiling sugar.

Flour.

Take the seven eggs, leaving out two whites. Whisk them well for a quarter of an hour, then add to them ½ lb. of boiling sugar. Whisk again for a quarter of an hour, then add 6 ozs. of flour. Mix lightly and bake.

Oatmeal Biscuits.

INGREDIENTS :

½ lb. of flour.
¼ lb. of dripping.
½ lb. of Scotch oatmeal.
Salt.   Water.

Put all the ingredients into a basin, and mix thoroughly with a little water into a paste. Roll out on a well-floured board very thin, and cut into rounds about the size of a penny. Bake in a quick oven for fifteen minutes. When cold, put them into a tin box, and they will keep good for a week or longer. They are very nice eaten with butter or cheese.

Hot Rolls for Breakfast. *(Very quickly made.)*

INGREDIENTS :

1 oz. of butter.
1 lb. of flour.
1 teaspoonful baking powder.
Pinch of salt.

Put the butter, flour, baking powder, and salt into a basin with enough milk to make a stiff dough. Mix well together, and drop in small lumps on a floured baking-tin (about the size of an egg). Bake in a good oven for about ten minutes.

Water Biscuits.

INGREDIENTS :

2 ozs. of butter.
½ lb. of flour.
Salt and water.

Rub the butter into the flour, add a good pinch of

salt. Mix with water into a dough, and roll out as soon as possible. Stamp with round cutters, prick, and put them in a not too quick oven and not too slow.

Cream Scones.

INGREDIENTS :

¾ lb. of flour.
1 teaspoonful baking powder.
1 oz. butter.
½ pint single cream.

Rub in the flour and baking powder and the butter, and make it all into a paste with the cream. Roll out quite thin and cut into rounds, and bake about four minutes on a hot grated gridle, turning the cakes only once. Split open when done, and put a lump of butter in each. Serve very hot.

Jersey Wonders.

INGREDIENTS :

3 ozs. of butter.
1 lb. of flour.
2 ozs. of caster sugar.
2 teaspoonfuls baking powder.
2 eggs.
Nutmeg.

Work the ingredients into a stiff paste, adding a little water if necessary. Roll out very thin, cut into strips, and plait or tie in fancy knots. Fry in deep, boiling fat which has been well clarified. Dry and sift sugar over them, and serve directly while they are hot.

Sponge Cake. (*Very good.*)

INGREDIENTS:

5 new-laid eggs.
¼ lb. of caster sugar.

6 ozs of flour.
Vanilla flavouring.

Break the eggs, and put the yolks into a basin and the whites in a soup-plate. Beat the yolks well, and then add the sugar and vanilla flavouring. Beat them up for fifteen minutes very lightly, then add the whites by degrees, beaten to a stiff froth, to the yolks in the basin. Keep beating the whole time. Beat all well together, and lastly sprinkle in the flour and keep beating until all is mixed. Have ready two 1 lb. tins, or three small moulds which have been oiled carefully and sprinkled with caster sugar and flour of equal quantities. Pour in the mixture, which must not be kept standing, so have moulds ready before beginning the cake. Bake in a nice hot oven for one hour; but do not put them at the top, but on the middle shelf, as they rise better. Before turning out, when done, leave in the tins for about three minutes, and be sure and leave them turned upside down on a sieve. Do not look in the oven for the first twenty minutes.

Rock Cakes.

INGREDIENTS:

½ lb. of flour.
½ teaspoonful baking powder.
4 ozs. of dripping.

2 ozs. of sugar.
2 ozs. of chopped peel.
4 ozs. of currants.

Mix the flour and baking powder, rub in the dripping, and add the currants, sugar, chopped peel, and the grated rind of one lemon. Mix to a very stiff paste with one egg and a little milk. Drop the mixture in very small lumps on a well-floured tin, and bake in a good oven.

Biscuits for Tea.

INGREDIENTS:

½ lb. flour.
¼ lb. butter.

2 ozs. caster sugar.

Rub the butter and sugar into the flour until quite smooth. Add a few drops of vanilla essence and water to make into a paste. Roll out very thin, and cut into rounds or fancy shapes. Bake in a hot oven for ten minutes.

Angelica and Cherry Cake.

INGREDIENTS:

5 ozs. of butter.
5 ozs. of sugar.
6 ozs. of flour.

3 ozs. of cherries.
2 ozs. of angelica.
3 eggs.

Put into a basin the butter and beat to a cream. Add the sugar, then beat well until smooth. Add the flour, cherries, and angelica. Mix the eggs in last, which must have been well whipped first. Thoroughly mix the cake, and put all into a well-buttered mould with a band of buttered paper round, and bake in a nice hot oven for about one hour.

Brighton Ginger-Cakes.

Ingredients:

Butter.
Eggs.
Flour.

Powdered ginger.
Loaf sugar.

Warm ½ lb. of butter, and beat up with four eggs, ½ lb. of flour, ½ lb. of powdered loaf sugar, and 2 ozs. of ginger mixed in by degrees. Roll out and cut into biscuits with a wineglass. Bake in a cool oven for twenty minutes.

Buns.

Ingredients:

6 ozs. of flour.
3 ozs. of butter.
3 ozs. of sugar.
2 ozs. of ground rice.

3 ozs. of currants.
1 egg.
Little milk and baking powder.

Beat the butter to a cream, and add the flour, sugar, rice, currants, and baking powder, then the egg beaten well, and mix all to a stiff paste with a little milk. Bake on a buttered baking-sheet in a hot oven for fifteen minutes. Brush over each bun with milk and sugar lightly.

Spanish Cakes.

Ingredients:

¼ lb. sweet almonds.
3 eggs (keeping out the whites of 2).

½ oz. bitter almonds.
¼ lb. of caster sugar.

Pound the almonds and sugar together, add the

eggs, and beat well. Bake the mixture in small dariole moulds. When quite cold put some thickly whipped cream on the top of each, and serve.

Chocolate Cake.

INGREDIENTS :

¼ lb. grated chocolate.
½ lb. sugar.

3 eggs.
¼ lb. fine flour.

Beat the yolks of the eggs first in a basin and add the sugar and chocolate. Beat well for ten minutes. Then add the whites of the eggs, which must be whipped to a stiff froth, lastly add the flour, and mix all well together. Put into a buttered, floured, and sugared fancy mould, and bake in a nice hot oven for one hour. This cake can be iced or not as liked.

Parmesan Biscuits.

INGREDIENTS :

Water biscuits.
Grated cheese.

Salt and pepper.
Butter.

Take the required number of water biscuits. Place on each a good heap of any grated cheese, and sprinkle over a pinch of salt and a good dust of pepper ; on the top place a few bits of butter. Then place them on a tin in a hot oven, and leave them until slightly browned. Serve while very hot.

Sark Sugar Cake.

INGREDIENTS:

1 lb. flour.	6 ozs. caster sugar or best
5 ozs. fresh butter.	Demerara.
½ oz. German yeast.	½ pint of warm water.

Put the flour into a basin and rub the butter with it, also the sugar. Then put the yeast in a basin and add the warm water. When the yeast is quite dissolved make a hole in the flour and put it in. Sprinkle a little of the flour over the liquid in the hole, put a clean cloth over the basin, and set it to rise in a warm place for one hour. Then knead well for five minutes, and make the dough up into two cakes. Place them in greased cake-tins, and set to rise again in the tins. When risen, bake them until done in a good oven, which will take about half an hour.

Yverdon Cakes.

INGREDIENTS:

1 lb. of finest flour.	2 or 3 eggs, according to the
¾ lb. of fresh butter.	paste.
¾ lb. of powdered sugar.	1 or 2 lemons (grated).

Beat the butter to a cream, add the flour, sugar, and lemons. Mix into a paste with the eggs, and drop in lumps on a buttered tin. Bake in a good oven.

Little Tea Cakes. (*Hol.*)

INGREDIENTS:

½ lb. of flour.
2 ozs. of butter.
1 oz. of caster sugar.

1 teaspoonful baking powder.
Little milk.

Mix all together in a basin and form into a dough with a little milk. Roll out on a pastry board about quarter inch thick. Cut into small rounds, or scone shape. Bake quickly in a hot oven. Split open when done, and butter well. Serve very hot.

Sultana Cake.

INGREDIENTS:

½ lb. flour.
¼ lb. caster sugar.
¼ lb. butter.
¼ lb. sultanas.

½ teaspoonful baking powder.
2 eggs.
Pinch of salt.
A little mixed peel.

Beat the butter to a cream, add the flour, caster sugar, sultanas, peel, baking powder, salt, and lastly the eggs, well beaten. Moisten with a little milk, if too stiff. Put all in a buttered cake-tin, and bake for one hour in a hot oven.

Aunt Sophy's Cake.

INGREDIENTS:

1 lb. butter.
1 lb. currants.
1 lb. raisins.
1½ lbs. flour.
6 eggs.
6 ozs. mixed peel.

1 lb. brown sugar.
1 teaspoonful of carbonate of soda.
1 nutmeg, grated, and rind of a lemon.
Wineglassful of brandy.

Beat the butter to a cream, and add the eggs

separately, and beat with the butter. Then add the fruit, picked and washed and dried, the sugar, soda, nutmeg, and lemon-rind, and last of all the flour and brandy. Put in a large buttered cake-tin, and bake in a hot oven for three hours.

Little Short-cakes.

INGREDIENTS :

1 lb. flour.
4 ozs. butter.
4 ozs. caster sugar.

1 egg.
1 gill of cream.

Rub the butter into the flour and sugar. Mix with one egg and a little cream. Form into a paste and roll out and cut into little rounds, and bake in a hot oven ten minutes. Split open and butter, if liked, or serve whole, hot.

Walnut Cake.

INGREDIENTS :

5 ozs. flour.
2 teaspoonfuls of baking powder.
¼ lb. of caster sugar.

¼ lb. of butter.
¼ lb. of chopped walnuts.
3 eggs.
Flavour with vanilla or orange

Cream the butter, add the caster sugar and the yolks of the eggs, well beaten, then the whites beaten to a stiff froth. Add the flour, walnuts, and baking powder, and a little milk. Have three round tins, well buttered, divide the mixture, and bake in a moderate oven for half an hour. When cold ice it all over, and decorate with whole halves of walnuts.

Imperial Cake.

INGREDIENTS :

1 lb. of butter.	2 teaspoonfuls of baking powder.
1 lb. of sugar.	9 eggs.
1 lb. of flour.	Juice of a lemon.
1 lb. of blanched almonds.	

Beat the butter to a cream, add the sugar, sift in the flour, and baking powder, then the lemon-juice. Beat the eggs well, and add the almonds last. Put into a large buttered cake-tin, and bake two hours. When cold ice it all over.

Orange Cake.

INGREDIENTS :

4 ozs. Vienna flour.	4 eggs.
2 teaspoonfuls of baking powder.	Grated rind of Seville orange. Juice of 2 sweet oranges.
6 ozs. of caster sugar.	

Cream the sugar and yolks of eggs for ten minutes with a wooden spoon. When thick add the rind and juice of the oranges. Then add the whites of the eggs, well beaten, and the flour. Bake from ten to twenty minutes. When cold put a layer of soft icing over the top, and decorate.

Soft icing.—Half a pound of icing sugar, and the juice of one orange. Beat well, and cover the cake. Line the tin, which should be about 1½ inches deep and about nine in diameter, with buttered paper.

Hot Water Sponge Cake.

INGREDIENTS:

2 cups of sugar.
2 cups of flour.
4 eggs.

2 teaspoonfuls of baking powder.

Half a cup of boiling water. Add this last.

Cocoanut Cake.

INGREDIENTS:

½ lb. of flour.
⅜ lb. of sugar.
¼ lb. of butter.
1 teaspoonful baking powder.
2 ozs. of cocoanut.

3 eggs.
1 teaspoonful of vanilla essence.
1 tablespoonful of milk.

Grate the cocoanut, and allow it to dry for two days. Beat the butter and sugar to a cream, then add milk. Beat the eggs until quite light, and add them. Shake in the flour and baking powder. Add the vanilla, and lastly the cocoanut, beating the mixture well, as each ingredient is added. Mix all well together, and put in a buttered cake tin. Bake in a gentle oven for an hour.

Ground Rice Cake.

INGREDIENTS:

1 lb. of flour.
5 ozs. of ground rice.
3 eggs.

5½ ozs. of caster sugar.
A little candied peel, and very little juice of lemon.

Beat the eggs first, then add the sugar, afterwards the flour, and other ingredients. Beat all together for twenty minutes or half an hour. Add the lemon-juice last.

XI
PRESERVES AND PICKLES

Jams.

I FIND all jams keep very good if made in the following way :—

Pick the fruit when quite dry, and when picked over or stoned (of course that depends on the fruit you are preserving) put the fruit into a large enamel or copper preserving-pan. Allow ¾ lb. of preserving sugar to every pound of fruit. Let the fruit boil for half an hour, and keep stirring all the time, then add the sugar, and let all boil for half an hour more. Then put into clean dry jam pots, and when cold tie down. If stoned fruit is being used stone it first, and crack the stones and put the kernels in with the fruit. It gives the jam a nice flavour.

Sloe Gin.

INGREDIENTS:

1 gallon of unsweetened gin.	3 lbs. lump sugar.
3 quarts of sloes.	3 ozs. bitter almonds.

Put in a two-gallon jar the sloes, sugar, almonds, and the gallon of gin. Shake it every day for two months. Then strain off and bottle. Cork down securely.

Cherry Brandy.

INGREDIENTS:

Morella cherries.
Best brandy.
Sugar candy.

Pick the Morella cherries when nearly black. See they are clean and dry. Prick each cherry a few times with a silver fork, and half fill wide-mouthed 2 lb. bottles with them and a little crushed sugar-candy, about ¼ lb. to a 2 lb. jar. Then fill up the bottles with best French brandy. Cork and put a bladder over them. This cherry brandy is delicious at Christmas time. It will keep good two or three years—the longer kept the stronger and better the brandy.

Orange Marmalade.

INGREDIENTS:

9 Seville oranges.
2 lemons.
Sugar.

Cut the fruit into thin slices, taking out all pips. To every pound of fruit add three pints of water. Let it stand twenty-four hours. Then boil until tender. Allow to stand until next day, and to every pound of fruit allow 1½ lbs. of sugar. Then boil until the chips are tender, usually about thirty minutes after it boils.

Blackberry Jelly.

INGREDIENTS:

Blackberries.
Preserving sugar.

Put all the blackberries in a large basin in a nice

PRESERVES AND PICKLES 161

hot oven until the juice runs from them freely. Then pour off the juice and press the fruit through a fine hair sieve until you have all the juice and pulp from the fruit, but not the pips. Allow 1 lb. of sugar to each pint of fruit, and boil altogether in an enamel or copper preserving pan for a quarter of an hour. Pour into little jelly pots, and when cold it will be perfectly firm. Tie down with paper.

Red-currant Jelly.

INGREDIENTS :

Red currants. | Loaf sugar.

Put the currants in a jar in the oven all night. Next morning squeeze the juice through a cloth over a fine hair sieve. Measure it, and to each pint of juice add 1 lb. of loaf sugar. Stir sugar and juice over the fire until it boils; watch it carefully, and let it boil for three minutes (hard). When it is done it will jelly most beautifully.

Chutney.

INGREDIENTS :

$\frac{1}{2}$ lb. sultanas. | $\frac{1}{2}$ pint vinegar.
$\frac{1}{2}$ lb. shallots. | 2 ozs. salt.
$\frac{1}{2}$ lb. sour apples, or gooseberries. | $\frac{1}{2}$ oz. of cayenne pepper.
 | $\frac{1}{2}$ lb. brown sugar.

Pound the whole together in a mortar, then gently boil until clear. Then put into glass jars and tie down with corks with bladder over.

Red Gooseberry Jam.

INGREDIENTS:

Gooseberries. | Preserving sugar.

Pick and top and tail the gooseberries, then weigh them, and to every 1 lb. of fruit allow ¾ lb. of sugar. Put the fruit into a preserving-pan (either copper or enamel) and stir them about until they boil. Let them boil for twenty minutes well, then add the sugar and let them boil again fast for half an hour. Keep stirring all the time. Take the pan off the fire and put the jam into clean dry jars or glass bottles. When cold it will be set firm. Then tie down with paper.

How to Tie Jam Down.

Cut some rounds of tissue paper the size of the insides of the pots, and dip them into brandy or whisky (one at a time). Place this paper on the fruit; then cut some more tissue paper a size larger than the pots. Have ready the white of an egg, well beaten, on a plate, and with a paste-brush smear over the egg on the paper and place over the jam pots. Press down the edges with a cloth. When dry the papers will be like parchment.

Rum Scrub.

INGREDIENTS:

3 eggs. | 1 tablespoonful of salad oil.
3 lemons. | ¼ lb. of barley sugar.
1 pint of best old rum. |

Let the eggs dissolve whole in the juice of the

three lemons (it will take about three days), turning them in the juice each day. When dissolved, or nearly so, beat them well up and remove any bits of shells. To this add one pint of best old rum, one tablespoonful of salad oil, and ¼ lb. of barley-sugar or sugar-candy. Mix all well together and keep in a corked bottle.

Dose.—One tablespoonful in half or a whole tumbler of milk on waking in the morning.

Pickle for Beef.

INGREDIENTS:

8 quarts water.
4 lbs. of salt.
1 oz. of saltpetre.
2 lbs. brown sugar.

2 ozs. peppercorns.
2 ozs. allspice.
1 oz. cloves.

Boil all the spices, salt, and sugar with the water well for about half an hour. Put the meat in the pickle, which must be cold, for a week, but the meat must first be put into cold water for two hours before putting it into the pickle. After the meat is pickled boil slowly, allowing twenty minutes for each pound.

Recipe for Preserving Eggs for Winter Use.

INGREDIENTS:

Eggs.
Cream of Tartar.

Salt.
Quicklime.

Put 2 lbs. of quicklime (buy it at the builder's) into a deep earthern pan. Pour over it two gallons of boiling water, and stir occasionally until quite cold. Then stir into it 1 oz. of cream of tartar, and 1 lb. of common salt. Thus eggs can be kept for six or eight months.

Cream Cheese (how to make).

Take one pint of thick sweet cream, tie it up in a piece of linen wetted in cold water. Let it hang for twelve hours then turn it out into a clean, wet cloth, and hang again for twelve hours. Put a piece of wetted butter muslin in a mould and press it in. Let it remain another twelve hours, then it is ready for market or use.

Egg Butter for Sandwiches.

INGREDIENTS :

| Eggs. | Butter. |
| Chili vinegar. | |

Boil two or three eggs hard. When cold peel and put them into a pestle and mortar. Pound up, adding butter, pepper, salt, and a few drops of chili vinegar. Put into a jam pot and pour a little oiled butter. This will keep good for a week and is very useful for afternoon tea sandwiches.

XII
USEFUL HINTS

(*WRINKLE*)

"A place for everything, and everything in its place."

Hints for Cooks.

BE down very early, not later than 6 a.m., so as to have plenty of time to get forward before breakfast.

All drawers and cupboards should be washed out and clean paper put on the shelves one day in every week, and all brights should be cleaned once a week.

All dishes for late dinner should be prepared as nearly as possible in the morning.

Never keep up a large fire unless absolutely necessary.

Never waste any pieces; a good cook can always find a use for all little scraps.

All doorsteps, both at front and back of house, should be cleaned before breakfast.

Cooks should always clear up as they go along, so as not to be in a muddle or late for meals—"A place for everything, and everything in its place."

Pastry should be made in the larder, as it is cooler than in the kitchen.

A kitchen should be kept quite tidy, as most dishes can be prepared in the scullery, if a nice large table is kept there.

Before going to bed leave everything washed up and put away in the kitchen and scullery quite tidy, so as you can begin straight away in the morning.

Hints for Parlourmaids.

Always make the breakfast, lunch, and dinner table look as nice as possible by having the plate, glass, and silver very bright and clean.

The secret of cleaning silver or plate is to have it washed in boiling water, soda, and yellow soap, or soft soap, and to rub very dry, and polish afterwards with a leather. A very little plate powder is needed if this is done.

All glasses should be washed in cold water, and polished with a cloth and dry leather afterwards.

Mind and see that the tablecloth and napkins are kept pressed in the linen-press and folded nicely ; and be sure the tablecloth is always put on the table quite straight and clean and in the centre of the table ; things put on crookedly spoil everything.

See that the plates for dinner and lunch are well rubbed up before they leave the kitchen.

Always open the front door to visitors as wide as possible, and if not at home wait with the door open until the visitors are quite clear of the house or garden.

Hints for Housemaids.

When cleaning out a room first brush all stuffed chairs, sofas, &c. Shake all cushions, table covers, and place all on a large sofa or chair and cover with a dust sheet. Then dust carefully all china ornaments that can be moved, photograph frames, books, little pictures that can be taken off the walls easily, and place together on a sofa, and cover over with another dust sheet. Then when all the pieces of furniture that dust will spoil are covered over, begin by shaking the curtains and pinning up carefully well off the floor. Sweep ceiling and walls with a soft broom, and tops of pictures and cupboards. Then sprinkle the carpets (of course all rugs and mats must be taken out into the garden and well shaken) with damp tea-leaves, and begin sweeping carefully all one way of the carpet, and take the dustpan and dust out of the room. Then clean your grate, blackleading it well while the dust is settling. Then remove the dust sheets carefully, so as not to let the dust fly about, and take them away. Next place the furniture where it should be in the room, and begin polishing it with furniture polish and elbow grease; then put back pictures, ornaments, &c., and lay down rugs, arrange curtains (after of course cleaning windows), and do not forget to dust doors, cornices, wainscotting, clean all silver and brasses in room, and leave everything quite clean and tidy, and pictures straight.

Never leave a room after sweeping and dusting without seeing that the windows have been rubbed, as dust settles on glass very quickly.

Never go up or downstairs empty-handed; if you work with your head you will save your legs.

See that there are pins and wax matches in all rooms, and do not leave dead flowers in rooms.

Water-bottles in bedrooms should be emptied every day, and refilled with fresh drinking-water.

To whiten a bath rub a little common whiting on the bath dry, and wash off and polish.

Always turn the hot or cold-water cans, when not in use, upside down, or if unable to do that leave the lids off always.

Always see before setting light to a fire that the register is open.

If lamps are not in daily use, be sure to wipe them carefully every day, as the oil oozes through, and makes a most unpleasant smell.

INDEX

I.—SOUPS.

	PAGE
A quickly made soup	11
Asparagus	10
Bonne Femme	9
Celery soup	6
Chestnut soup	13
Clear soup	4, 13
Conger soup	9
Green-pea soup	13
How to keep a good stock-pot	3
Onion soup (white)	12
Oxtail soup	5
Palestine soup	6
Potage à la Monte Carlo	8
Potage à la Provençale	8
Potato soup	10
Soubise soup (white)	7
Tapioca soup	12
Tomato soup	7
White soup with macaroni	11

II.—FISH.

	PAGE
Brandade of cod	19
Cod à la capers	26
Dried haddock	30
Duncroft soles	30
Filleted plaice	28
Fillets of sole à l'Italienne	29
Fish à la Jess	28
„ à la Mièville	20
„ au gratin	27
„ castles	25
„ mould	24
„ pie	18
Fried fillets of lemon sole	18
Grilled whiting	18
Haddock balls	23
„ sauté	24
How to cook salmon	31
„ fry smelts	26
Lobster cutlets	23
Oyster soufflé	20
Salmon creams	21
„ mayonnaise	22
Sole à la Cannes	19
„ „ Nice	27
„ „ Paine	29
To use up remains of cold fish	21
Whitebait	17
Whiting à la Horsell	26

III.—ENTRÉES.

	PAGE
Bantams' eggs in aspic	40
Braised lamb cutlets au purée de marrow	46
Chicken croquettes	51
,, cutlets	36
Crepinettes of lobster, game, or chicken	42
Curried eggs	51
Cutlets à la Diable	46
,, ,, Milanaise	50
Egg kromiskies	51
Fillets of beef	35
,, ,, and mushrooms	43
How to serve prawns for lunch	44
How to cook sweetbreads	48
Jubilee kidneys	39
Kidneys in bacon	47
Kidney slices	49
Kidney toast	44
Larded oysters on mushrooms	53
Little fancy chicken or game moulds	37
Little tit-bits	50
Lobster à la Mont Fleury	43
Marrow moulds	45
Mushrooms à la Margaretta	52
Œufs à la tongue	53
Œufs poches au asperge	41
Oxtail à la Cannes	37
Oysters in cases	41
,, in mayonnaise	42
Pigeons in cases	38
Salines of chicken or partridge	47
Savoury hashed mutton	45
Stuffed larks	36
Sweetbread fritters à la Claudine	49
Sweetbread soufflé	48
Sweetbreads à la Hatch	39
Vol-au-vent à la Toulouse	40

IV.—JOINTS AND SIDE DISHES.

	PAGE
A nice way of doing up cold meat à la Toodles	62
Beef and rice	63
Boiled chicken	65
,, leg of mutton	58
Boned roast pigeons	64
Cold pressed beef	59
Collared head or brawn	61
Devilled mutton slices	67
Fillet of beef (larded)	60
Good breakfast dish	62
How to boil pork	62
,, roast an old fowl	66
,, use up cold mutton	68
,, make three small joints out of a sirloin of beef	59
Mutton à la Paine	66
,, balls	68
Pigeon pudding	64
Pope patties	63
Rolled loin of mutton	58
,, spiced beef	57
,, stuffed steak	60
Stuffed boned neck of lamb	61

V.—VEGETABLES AND SALADS.

	PAGE
Asparagus	74
Baked potatoes	78
,, tomatoes	77
Beetroot	75
,, and celery salad	79
Cucumber and tomato salad	79
French bean salad	81
,, beans boiled whole	73

INDEX

	PAGE
French salad	80
Haricot beans	74
„ purée	74
How to cook carrots and turnips	73
How to cook mushrooms	75
„ „ new potatoes	77
„ keep French beans or scarlet runners	76
Lobster salad à la Maude	79
Mushrooms as a vegetable	81
My salad	80
Orange salad	78
Potato balls	74
„ croquettes	76
„ scallops	77
Potatoes for breakfast	78
Salad dressing	80
Shrimp or prawn salad	81
Spinach	75
Stuffed tomatoes	82
Vegetable marrow (how to cook)	73
Young early carrots	75

VI.—PUDDINGS AND SWEETS.

Apricots à la Snow	98
„ and rice	92
A quickly made sweet	103
Baked apple pudding	87
„ cream	95
„ plum-pudding	96
„ suet pudding under the meat	94
Bread pudding	92
Chocolate pudding	101
Christmas pudding (the best)	100
Custard in jelly	102

	PAGE
Dried pippin apples	96
French plum-pudding	95
Golden drops	88
Green plum tart	89
Jubilee pudding	97
Lemon cheesecakes	102
Lop-lollie	99
Marigolds	100
Meringues	91
Miniature rice moulds	97
Pear charlotte	90
Pear meringue	85
Pears in cream	89
Petits château de trois colours	93
Prune shape	93
Puff pastry	86
Raspberries and cream	94
Rice and pears	90
Short-crust, for, cakes or tarts	85
Sayer's plum-pudding	86
Sponge cake castles	88
Strawberries and cream in winter	97
Swiss roll	101
Tapioca cream	98
Urney pudding	103
Yorkshire pudding	94
Zephyrs of semolina	99

VII.—SAVOURIES.

Aigrettes of Parmesan	112
Anchovy cream savoury	113
„ parcels	119
Cauliflower au gratin	119
Cheese biscuits or cheese straws	113
Cheese marbles	115
„ sticks	108

	PAGE		PAGE
Chicken liver savoury	111	Windsor sauce	129
Cod's roe	109	Horseradish sauce	125
Croûtes à la Clarisse	114	Icing for Genoese pastry	123
Devilled sardine butter	116	Mayonnaise sauce	132
„ shrimps	111	Ordinary thick brown sauce	130
Egg and tomato savoury	117	Piquant sauce	130
Eggs and anchovies	108	Plain syrup for stewing whole fruit	123
Fried sardines	107	Sauce for fish	132
Ham and egg toast	117	„ for ragout of cold game	125
Macaroni and tomatoes	115	„ for rice moulds	128
„ cheese	117	„ haddock	127
Moelle de bœuf aux tomates	114	„ Hollandaise	128
Mushrooms and marrow on toast	109	Savoury custard	124
Œufs à la Brentmore	116	Shrimp sauce	130
Olives à la Métropole	114	Tar-Tar sauce	129
Prawns and mayonnaise	110	To clarify dripping	124
Prawns and anchovy butter	110	Tomato sauce for keeping	126
Ramequins	120	„ sauce	127
Sardines à la surprise	111	Toosie sauce	130
„ „ Toby	118	White sauce	131
Scrambled sardines	118	Wine sauce for puddings	125
Shrimps and green butter	108		
„ à la mayonnaise	110	IX. Hors d'Œuvres.	
Tomato savoury	107	Anchovy tastes	135
To use up eggs	120	Anchovies	137
Yellow and green butter baskets	112	Bloater roes	138
		Caviare	138
VIII.—Sauces, Icings, &c.		Devilled prawns	139
Batter for frying	124	German sausage	135
Brandy cream sauce	126	Lobster pots	136
Bread sauce	131	Oysters	138
Chocolate glaze	123	Sardine creams	136
„ icing	123	Sardines à la Royal	137
Caramel	128	Tomato cups	136
"Donna Lol" sauce	129		
Dutch sauce	126	X.—Fancy Breads, Cakes, and Biscuits.	
Egg sauce	131	Angelica and cherry cake	149
		Aunt Sophy's cake	153

INDEX

	PAGE		PAGE
Biscuits for tea	149	Sultana cake	153
Bread	143	Walnut cake	154
Brighton ginger-cakes	150	Water biscuits	146
Buns	150	Yverdon cakes	152
Chocolate cake	151		
Cocoanut cake	156	XI.—Preserves and Pickles.	
Cream scones	147	Blackberry jelly	160
Duncroft cakes	144	Cherry brandy	160
Gingerbread cake	145	Chutney	161
Ground rice cake	156	Cream cheese	164
Hot rolls for breakfast	146	Egg butter	164
Hot-water sponge cake	156	How to tie jam down	162
Imperial cake	155	Jams	159
Jersey wonders	147	Orange marmalade	160
Little queen cakes	144	Pickle for beef	163
„ short cakes	154	Recipe for preserving eggs	163
„ tea cakes	153	Red-currant jelly	161
Madeira cake	145	Red gooseberry jam	162
Oatmeal biscuits	146	Rum scrub	162
Orange cake	155	Sloe gin	159
Parmesan biscuits	151		
Rock cakes	148	XII.—Useful Hints.	
Sark sugar cake	152		
Spanish cakes	150	Hints for Cooks	167
Sponge cake	145	„ Parlourmaids	168
„ (very good)	148	„ Housemaids	168

UNWIN BROTHERS, THE GRESHAM PRESS, WOKING AND LONDON